THE **PRIVATE GARDENS** OF SMI LANDSCAPE ARCHITECTURE

THE **PRIVATE GARDENS** OF SMI LANDSCAPE ARCHITECTURE

Edited by
Jorge Sánchez

MERRELL
LONDON • NEW YORK

CONTENTS

PREFACE Jorge Sánchez

It is said that it takes a village to make a child. SMI is our village: we all make it so, and it makes us. Landscape gardening has been our discipline for a few decades; it took us a long time to have an office where projects move as smoothly as they do now, and many years to gain the experience we have. It took a long time to form a group where "things click," where we all work for one another.

This book shows how not one individual but many make a firm successful. We have reached the point where those who were project managers are now a very strong element of the design team; where the CAD operator can express his creative self and benefit us all; where an assistant can actually assist and support; where a bookkeeper can allow the rest to perform where their talents are put to best use.

This book is dedicated to our interpretation of our clients' needs and desires. We feel strongly that we are here to interpret our clients' dreams, and since each client is different, those challenges make our design work fun. No project is ever the same as any other. Our designs cover different planting zones, and that too makes them all the more challenging and interesting.

I have always felt that traveling is the best education for a gardener. Seeing variety—not just in gardens, but also culturally, historically, and architecturally—brings us closer to a wider idea of design. I hope this book, with the many different spaces it illustrates, will give the reader that spark of variety and experience.

CASA BENDITA

Claudia Visconti Clippinger, Senior Associate

Steven Brooke, Photographer

When working on a garden, there are many aspects that designers prioritize and consider carefully. The two most influential, of course, are the site itself and the client. The environmental and geographical conditions of the site and how it will be used dictate the overall form of the garden. It seems that what the site fails to determine, the client does, and vice versa. I find that a garden is most successful when it reflects the character of its owner and the house's architecture. Casa Bendita exemplifies both these principles. Its owners, Sophie Desmarais and Daniel Valoatto, are fantastic hosts and love to entertain, and that is reflected in the layout, function, and furnishings of their garden.

The name of the couple's home is deeply rooted in the history of the site. In 1912, Henry S. Phipps, partner and accountant of Andrew Carnegie for Carnegie Steel, purchased 1,000 feet of oceanfront in Palm Beach, Florida, and gifted it to his children. It was only a few years later that the children subdivided the lots into three parcels. A house was subsequently built on each parcel. Henry's son John built his—the most beautiful of the three, some say—after the First World War, and named it Casa Bendita. Its coquina tennis gazebo was preserved for many years in the center of the cul-de-sac, until it became hazardous and beyond repair. Most recently, the gazebo has been re-created as an overlook in Bradley Park, Palm Beach. Since a wall from the original estate, designed by the resort architect Addison Mizner, remains in the garden, it seemed appropriate to continue the legacy in the name.

1. MOTOR COURT
2. TERRACE
3. POOL TERRACE
4. BATHROOM GARDEN

Dwarf water lilies are surrounded by a sward of diamond Zoysia grass, backed with a hedge of Ficus nitida *and the bamboo palm,* Chamaedorea seifrizii; Gardenia jasminoides *"Miami Supreme" is beyond.*

MOTOR COURT

Framed by hedges and a pair of urns on pilasters, the entry gives views of the pebble and simulated-stone motor court from the road. The court is laid out in a diamond pattern, with black river stones placed as the joints for the coral stone. Thin borders of river stones delineate the main parking court and the secondary drive space. Each river stone was placed by hand to ensure that all were cohesive in size and laid flush. Turning into this parking area, visitors are greeted by a Buddha statue that appears to float above a rectangular pool of water lilies. It is flanked by a pair of large *Ficus aurea* trees that arch together overhead. *Chamaedorea* palms planted behind the Buddha enhance the Asian effect and frame the statue in a more intimate way. A *Ficus nitida* hedge runs along the eastern property line, providing a simple backdrop to this serene setting and screening the neighbors' property from view.

A beautifully scented *Trachelospermum jasminoides* (confederate jasmine) is espaliered on the low retaining walls between the elevated house and the lower motor court, and two large date palms on either side of the entrance give a strong focal point on the axis of the motor court. Steps lined with small pots lead to the front door, which is further framed by two large black urns planted with *Bougainvillea*. The dark furnishings and architectural features provide a strong contrast to the muted coral stone, adding drama to the entrance.

To the left, a pair of 6-foot black AZEK gates (a proprietary, low-maintenance wood alternative), made in a lattice to match the garden gates, encloses the service parking space. This parking area has the same diagonal pattern as the motor court, minus the joints of river stone. It is accessed from the sidewalk via a stepping-stone path, which allows easy service to and from the street without going through the garden.

The front entry is of simulated stone and Mexican river stones. The trunk of a Ficus aurea *is visible in the left foreground; Confederate jasmine (*Trachelospermum jasminoides*) is trained on the low wall and the steps are lined with* Podocarpus *and* Carmona *hedges. The Medjool date palm (*Phoenix dactylifera*) is underplanted with the white* Begonia *"Odorata Alba" and* Bismarckia nobilis.

TERRACE

Sophie and Daniel enjoy a lively social life, so their rear garden is centered on entertainment. Walking from the house onto the large rear terrace, you first come under an awning with a small table and comfortable sofas, offering shade for relaxation. Beyond is a fire pit surrounded by four large white chairs. The entertainment setting continues with another table, this one much larger, for dining by the pool. Sophie is an avid lover of urns, and all tables are decorated with examples that she has collected during her travels. Among her favorites are blue-and-white porcelain ginger jars from Asia. Urns and pots also surround this space, lining the steps up to the doors and offering accents among the planting beds. To soften the house and terrace, planters were placed along the walls of the house, filled with *Asystasia gangetica* (Ganges primrose) and columns of *Elaeocarpus*. The strong presence of urns in the garden is unique to this home and reflects the interest of the client. It is always fun to be presented with a distinctive element by the client, and to design the garden to allow these components to speak strongly without looking misplaced. Niches in the garden and steps wide enough to accommodate the urns created the perfect environment for the client's decorative collection to become part of the landscape. Planting some of the urns and allowing others to remain empty added to the aesthetic of the garden without overwhelming the other features.

Pages 14–15: Wall-trained Stephanotis floribunda *and columns of* Podocarpus macrophyllus *are underplanted with the white* Begonia *"Odorata Alba" and framed with a hedge of* Carmona microphylla.

Left: The garden terrace is backed by the historic estate wall.

POOL TERRACE

Running east–west, the pool is perpendicular to the house, on an asymmetrical axis with the front door. Its rectangular shape is interrupted by semicircles at each end planted with multistemmed *Adonidia* palms, underplanted with *Trachelospermum asiaticum* (jasmine minima). It is fitting that these palms should be flanked by black urns planted with the false agave, *Furcraea foetida*. Four chaise longues furnish the terrace. The original Phipps estate wall, which remains on the Casa Bendita property, forms a backdrop to the rear garden, running parallel to the pool and providing a focal point on an axis with the front door. The wall is lined with a rhythm of columnar *Podocarpus macrophyllus* (Japanese yew) and large urns with espaliered *Stephanotis floribunda* behind them. The espaliers look as though they are coming out of the urns, yet the urns are in fact empty. *Begonia* "Odorata Alba" is planted loosely in front of the urns and columns, and a contrasting small, tight hedge of *Carmona microphylla* borders the bed. A beautiful purple bougainvillea, *B.* "New River," adorns the western portion of the wall, for color and contrast.

At the west end of the pool is a small terrace lined with chaises longues and a large umbrella, and beyond it a daybed on a stone pad in the grass. Wicker tables with ginger jars sit on each side. In the background, a series of hedges are trained to create niches, which give a sense of division to the space. On either side of the daybed is a half-moon bed of gardenia underplanted with jasmine minima, with central tall white urns containing *Sansevieria cylindrica*, an erect succulent.

To the north, bougainvillea densely covers an exterior wall, around a window with a blue-and-white urn on the sill. This green wall softens the building's relationship to the rear garden and pool, and offers a scenic background for a pair of chairs and an ottoman, adding to the seating available for entertaining.

Walls of Bougainvillea *"New River" overlook the sun terrace, with low* Carmona microphylla *hedges, and conical columns of* Elaeocarpus *are underplanted with* Philodendron *"Burle Marx.". By the pool, groups of* Adonidia *palm are surrounded by* Trachelospermum asiaticum *(jasmine minima).*

An AZEK gate in a wall of Bougainvillea *"New River" leads to the bathroom garden. On the walls hang white orchids,* Vanda rothschildiana.

BATHROOM GARDEN

Hidden from the main part of the rear garden is a walled-in courtyard with a spectacular collection of orchids and, of course, urns. The stucco wall that it shares with the rear garden is espaliered with confederate jasmine in a diamond pattern, to soften it and make the courtyard feel more like a garden. An arched gate of black trelliswork closes off the wall. Tall hedges of *Podocarpus* with a foreground of black lattice panels wall in the northern and eastern sides of the Bathroom Garden, and the house is to the south. *Ptychosperma macarthurii* palms occupy the northeastern corner, anchoring the space and softening its orthogonal geometry.

This courtyard is floored with a continuation of the diamond pattern found in the rest of the rear garden, so that the two spaces speak the same language but still feel like different "rooms." A set of comfortable chairs with an ottoman and an umbrella offer a quiet escape from the pool terrace, which is often busy. Remarkable Vanda orchids—most of them white or purple—hang from the lattice walls, contrasting with the strong black trellis. More blue-and-white porcelain ginger jars appear here, perhaps more than in any other part of the garden, and the varying shades of blue provide color among the light-hued paving and furnishings. This unexpected space is accessible from the master bath, so it is a focal point from the master suite as well as a private space for the clients even when they have guests.

FISHER GARDEN

Brian Vertesch, Senior Associate

Steven Brooke, Photographer

Jeff and Frances Fisher had bought a large vacant lot in the middle of Palm Beach and had contracted SMI to design the gardens for their new project—our third collaboration with them. We were well into the project and close to obtaining approval from the Town Architectural Review Commission when Frances phoned us out of the blue and asked if we could meet her at a new property they had just purchased in the town. It was a beautiful, though somewhat run-down, house designed in 1926 by John Volk, a renowned architect in the history of Palm Beach. Frances explained that she and Jeff had always admired the house, and could not pass up the opportunity when it came on the market. After a quick tour of the house and existing garden, Frances asked us to stop work on the current project and start on concepts for the new garden, thus beginning our fourth collaboration with the couple.

Frances quickly accumulated a large dossier of historic photographs and other information relating to the property, and she shared it with us and with the architectural firm, Clemens Bruns Schaub, that she hired to do the architectural restoration. With this information in hand, the Fishers wasted little time in determining that the facades should be returned to Volk's original design. The discussion of the garden revolved around the history of the house's different garden spaces, most of which had been changed many times since it was first made, and gardens that the Fishers admired, some of which they had recently visited on a trip to Italy.

Having studied the historical and architectural significance of the house, and already being very familiar with how the Fishers would plan to use the garden, we quickly established our approach. We would create a series of formal and informal spaces, all of which would blur the line between interior and exterior. Each garden space would be shielded slightly from the next, providing glimpses of the spaces beyond, which would draw visitors further into the garden and allow them to slowly discover the elements of each. The Fishers were active participants throughout the development of our designs, and in fact also throughout the project, from concept to completion, and their passion for the whole restoration was always evident. We believe this shows in the wonderful result.

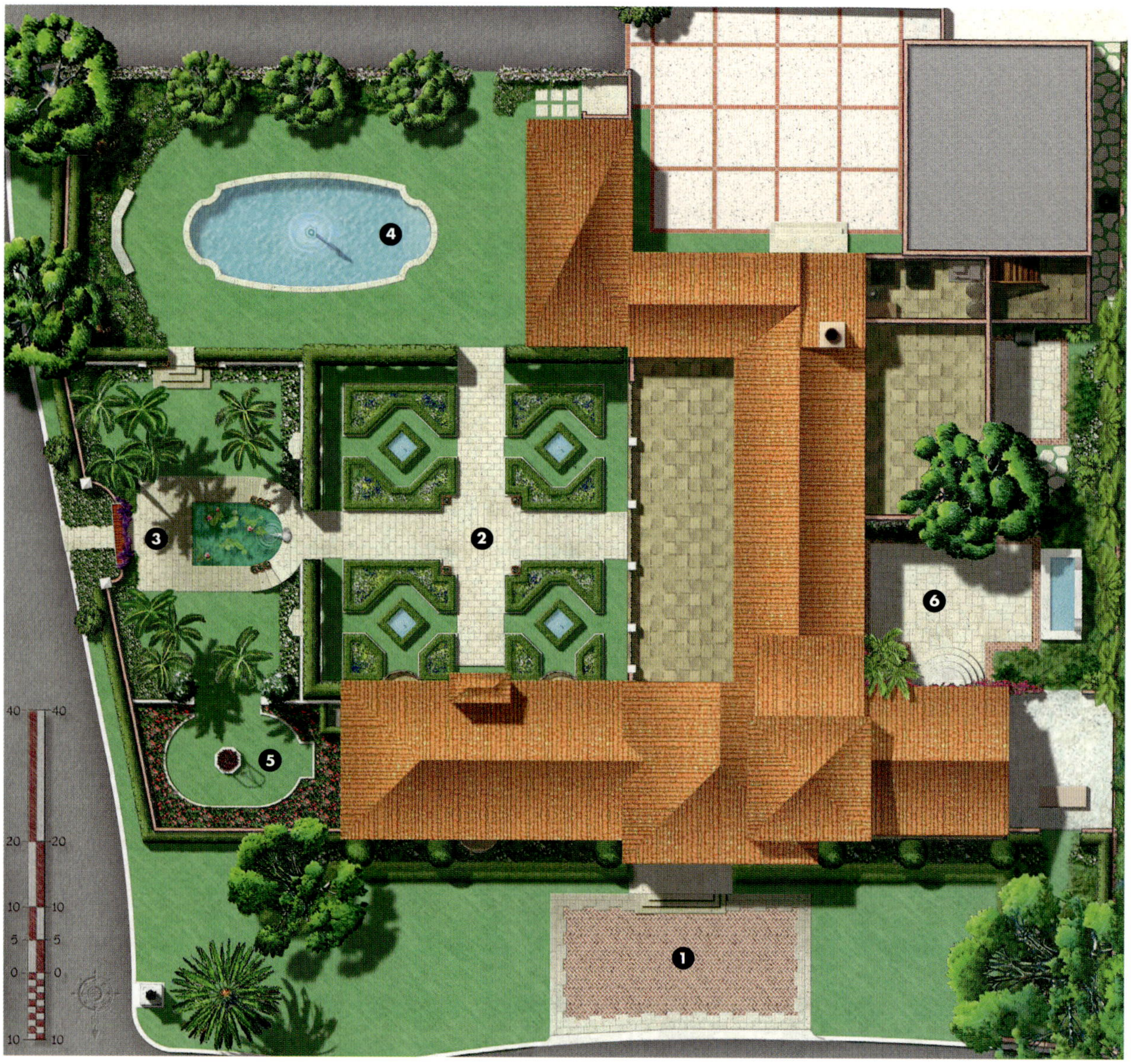

1 FRONT ENTRY
2 COURTYARD GARDEN
3 KOI POND GARDEN
4 SWIMMING POOL GARDEN
5 ROSE GARDEN
6 DINING GARDEN

Custom-made terra-cotta jars mark the boundary between Swimming Pool Garden and Koi Pond Garden. Roystonia regia *palms are arranged in a naturalistic grove, and* Agave americana *in terra-cotta pots top new pilasters that mark the entrance to the Rose Garden beyond.*

FRONT ENTRY

We removed the existing driveway and plantings that obscured views of the front facade. We developed a large yet simple parking court with a minimalist planting plan in order to direct the focus to the strong architectural elements of the house. Just as the house is historic, the road that leads to it was designed before guidelines came into force that require wider pavement sections, and although the narrower roads are much more attractive, maneuvering into and out of driveways on this street can be difficult. As well as functioning aesthetically for the house, the simple design of the parking court makes parking much easier. The paved surfaces are of reclaimed Chicago brick and coral stone. A garden path of coral stone and grass connects the street to the main entry, although it is reinforced to accommodate vehicles if necessary. An existing pair of Japanese yew columns (*Podocarpus macrophyllus*) terminate the facade at each end, with white tropical begonias and *Ligustrum* topiary between. At each end of the front garden, a large tree frames the house further. An existing African tulip tree (*Spathodea campanulata*) anchors the east end of the front garden, and a magnolia was transplanted from behind the house to anchor the west end of the front garden.

The entrance to the house leads to a central dining room that opens to two different gardens, one on each side of the house. Realizing that visitors to this room would be able to see both the eastern and the western garden at the same time, we varied the styles to create an interesting juxtaposition. To the east is a formal courtyard garden influenced by the Italian Renaissance gardens that the Fishers had visited, while to the west is a more relaxed tropical garden centered on a new wall fountain.

A large Spathodea campanulata *tree anchors the corner of the house, and* Begonia *"Odorata Alba,"* Podocarpus macrophyllus *"Pringles," and spheres of* Ligustrum lucidum *(Chinese privet) are planted formally at the base of the walls.*

In the Courtyard Garden, coral-stone walkways are bordered by reclaimed Chicago brick. Podocarpus macrophyllus *"Pringles" forms the low parterres, infilled with seasonal flowers, and also the tall hedges with arched openings.*

COURTYARD GARDEN

During our first meeting at the new house, Frances expressed her desire for a courtyard-style garden. As we developed concepts for the garden to the east of the dining room, entered from the loggia, we began to formulate a plan to create a courtyard-like space by using two of the existing house walls and introducing two tall "green walls" of Japanese yew. Arches trained into the hedges echo those of the loggia and provide views of the Koi Pond and Swimming Pool gardens beyond. Since planting is always the last thing to be done during construction, we started training and growing the arches at the plant nursery of the landscape contractor, Botanica Landscaping, while house and garden were under construction. That meant we could eventually install hedge arches that looked much more established than if we had waited until the end of construction, as is often done.

In order to obscure the view through the open arches slightly, and to create a mystery about what lies beyond, we added tall terra-cotta pots containing small flowering trees, which also act as accents. Two coral-stone walks cross the courtyard, dividing it into four fountain gardens, each a formal parterre with a small lotus fountain at the center. The soft sound of trickling water permeates this part of the garden.

A view from the koi pond toward the rear loggia. Here, too, the parterre hedges are of Podocarpus macrophyllus *"Pringles."*

In the Koi Pond Garden, coral-stone steps and wall veneer form the shape of the pond. Arched Podocarpus macrophyllus *hedges extend from the central axis and are accentuated with terra-cotta pots and miniature balconies, all underplanted with* Begonia *"Odorata Alba."*

KOI POND GARDEN

Looking from the loggia down the walkway that bisects the courtyard, one sees the back of a clam shell that sits atop a drop-off, hiding the garden below. The drop-off, created by a retaining wall and steps, is a version of the ha-has used throughout history to separate gardens from livestock beyond, while maintaining a scenic view. The shell invites the visitor to move into the next garden, and as they approach it, the Koi Pond Garden is revealed.

The koi pond was originally designed as a fountain, but the Fishers asked us to modify the details of the basin to accommodate koi fish, since the pond was to be a special element for their son. The aesthetic changes that were required to accommodate the koi were minimal; most of the work that had to be done was in the filtration and treatment of the water. The walls and steps are all made from coral stone. Small terra-cotta pots, rather than a railing, create a buffer between the pond and the water, giving a much more open and enjoyable view of the area from both the Koi Pond Garden and the loggia. Tropical water lilies, both day- and night-blooming, were added for their beauty and to provide shelter for the koi. Royal palms (*Roystonia regia*) were moved from the driveway and planted informally in the lawns next to the pond. Adjacent to the pond steps, two balconettes extend from the arched hedges, allowing a view of the Koi Pond Garden from the formal parterres above. The railings on the balconettes mimic the original ones designed by Volk for this house. Terminating the view from the loggia over the Koi Pond Garden is a fabulous portal with a double gate that is original to the Volk design and was refurbished as part of the project.

Terra-cotta pots containing seasonal flowers form a barrier between steps and pond. Waterlilies, both day- and night-blooming, provide beauty and shelter for the fish.

SWIMMING POOL GARDEN

This garden can be accessed from both the Koi Pond Garden and the Courtyard Garden. From the former, we opened a space in an existing balustrade that separated the pond from the pool garden, and added a set of coral-stone steps. On each side of the steps, we placed a pair of decorative terra-cotta pots that were made specially for one of the Fishers' earlier gardens. From the parterre, the pool garden is accessed down one of the central walkways. In another change of planting style, the pool garden is much more relaxed and tropical. Rather than surrounding the pool with paving, we added a firm *Zoysia* lawn that creates a much softer pool area and gives the swimming pool the appearance of a fountain, an effect that is amplified by the retractable fountain spout in the middle of the pool and the decorative coral-stone coping. A canvas awning covers an outdoor seating area with barbecue equipment at one end of the pool, while an antique stone trellis, statue, and bench anchor the other end of the garden. Flowering vines were trained over the antique stone, and flowering trees and shrubs create an attractive backdrop. *Ficus lyrata* (fiddleleaf fig) trees were used next to the pool on one side to provide privacy where the property is closest to the neighbors. On the other borders of the pool garden, hedges of Japanese yew provide privacy at a lower level while allowing views of relocated royal palms and some of the more decorative architectural elements of the adjacent houses.

Coral-stone steps lead from the Koi Pond Garden to the Swimming Pool Garden, through a new opening created in an existing balustrade.

The pool has a coral-stone coping and steps, and is finished with blue glass tile. A retractable fountain spout adds movement and sound.

ROSE GARDEN

On one of our visits during construction, we were asked to consider a space for roses, which are not the easiest plant to grow in Palm Beach. As we walked around the site to consider where we might place them, we discovered an opportunity for a new garden area that we had not yet considered. At the opposite end of the Koi Pond Garden from the Swimming Pool Garden, we removed a wall and extended the garden toward the street. In doing so we were able to create another long axis through the garden, accentuating the length of the property. The extension reclaimed an area of the property that was public and gave the area back to the private garden. We moved an existing decorative well into this new private area, to serve as a focal point from the dining room and from the Koi Pond and Swimming Pool garden steps. A pair of pilasters marks the entrance to the new Rose Garden, and supports climbing roses.

DINING GARDEN

On the opposite side of the house from the Courtyard Garden, we created a very different kind of garden. From the house, the main view of the Dining Garden is across a paved area to a rustic limestone wall fountain surrounded by tropical plants. Different leaf sizes, textures, and shapes create attractive layers and a tropical ambiance. Splashes of color were added with more small terra-cotta pots, both on the fountain wall and on the steps that lead from the house.

Another repeated design element is the brick and coral stone that were also used for the driveway and Courtyard Garden walkways.

Bougainvillea and *Trachelospermum jasminoides* cover the house walls here, and a very large *Bursera simaruba* (gumbo-limbo tree) was moved in to give shade and interest, with its sculptural trunk. The central paved area can accommodate large or small gatherings while maintaining a charming sense of scale.

A large limestone fountain anchors the Dining Garden, and the property line is screened with a tall hedge of Clusia guttifera. *The borders are filled with tropical* Heliconia *and* Musa acuminata *Cavendish Group, whose large leaves provide vertical interest, and varieties of* Alocasia *and* Monstera deliciosa.

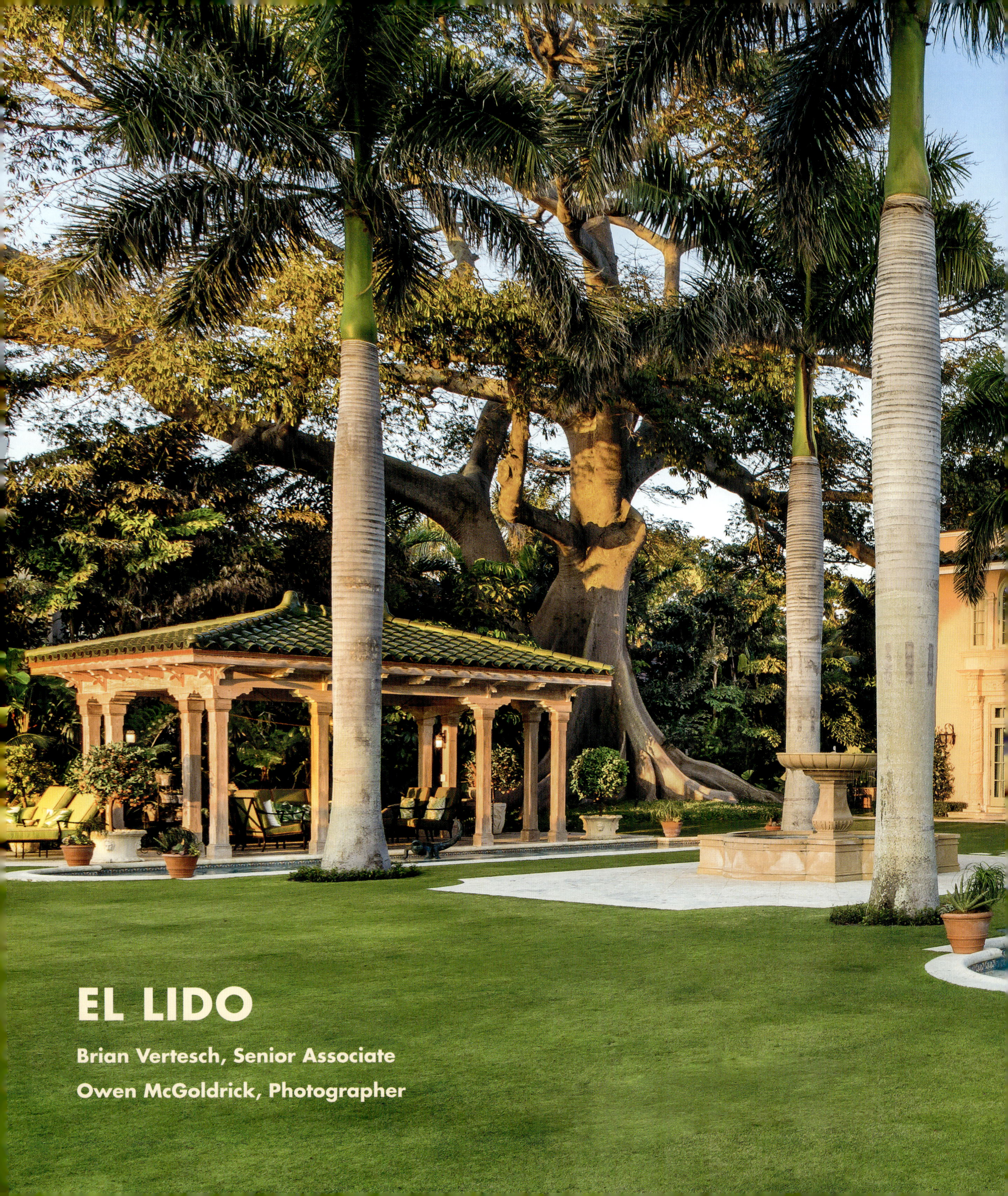

EL LIDO

Brian Vertesch, Senior Associate

Owen McGoldrick, Photographer

Deborah and Charles (Chuck) Royce were undertaking renovations at El Lido—their historic home on the Lake Trail, just north of the middle bridge in Palm Beach—when they contacted SMI for assistance in renovating the gardens. We found a very interestingly shaped house at the end of a quiet dead-end street. The half-hexagon shape of the front of the house made a big first impression, as this is not a common shape for houses in South Florida. Apart from that, however, the front court was unattractive and dominated by a sea of concrete paving. A large *Ficus* hedge separated the front court from the street, and a group of palms further blocked views of the front of the house from the road. The facade nevertheless had great potential.

We were met by the Royces and Jacqueline Albarran, a Palm Beach architect with whom we have worked many times very successfully. It turned out that the plan was to bring many elements of the front facade back to the original design, which was completed in about 1920. As we discussed the proposed changes to the house and how they might affect the front gardens, I remembered passing the house as a boy and noticing the green tiles on the roof. That resulted in the use of green tiles—rather unusually—as part of the refurbishment.

As we emerged into the lakeside garden, we found ourselves in the shadow of an awesome giant kapok (*Ceiba pentandra*) on the edge of the property. Its roots are raised above the ground, up to 4 feet in some places, and extend almost 50 feet from the trunk in all directions. The rest of the garden appeared to be a mix of elements that had been added at various times. An *allée* of *Roystonia regia* (royal palm) appeared to be original, while the pool and hardscape looked to have been added in the last twenty years. We found the rear terraces and steps very uncomfortable. To enter the garden from the rear loggia, we had to descend several steep sets of steps. We also found that the many layers between the loggia, pool, and garden made the garden feel much smaller than it was. Level changes and access would be one of the main aspects for us to address.

Deborah and Chuck explained their wishes for the garden, which included an open-air pool cabana, which Jackie would be developing. Understanding that the cabana would be a prominent feature of the garden, we convinced everyone that it should be placed near the northern property line, where it would be most protected from the winter winds. We felt this location, near the kapok, would be a much more dramatic place for it.

With a clear understanding of the architecture and our clients' program, we began working on what would turn out to be a wonderful garden that accentuates the architecture and somewhat unusual shape of the house, as well as creating seamless connections between the interior rooms and the adjacent garden spaces.

1 FRONT DRIVE
2 LAKESIDE GARDEN
3 TWO POOLS
4 LAKE TRAIL ACCESS

FRONT DRIVE

Knowing that the front facade of the house would be returned to its more attractive original design, and that the dead-end street in front has little traffic, we decided to open the front gardens to the street. We removed the *Ficus* hedge at the front of the property, and the palms in the center of the drive, and replaced the concrete with a simple horseshoe-shaped drive. The sides of the drive follow the angle of each wing of the house. To provide an attractive view of the road from the front door, a *Ficus* tree was moved from the front corner of the garden to be centered with the door. Two others were trucked in and planted on the opposite side of both driveway legs, to create a tunnel over each entrance. Beyond the tunnel, the planting is lower and allows in light and open views of the house. The planting directly by the house is formal, and consists of a perimeter *Carmona microphylla* hedge and *Ptychosperma macarthurii* (Macarthur palm) underplanted with flowering tropical begonias.

Developing the hardscape for the entry drive, as well as other areas, we specified materials that would complement the historical nature of the house. Coral stone, which is used on many historic houses in Palm Beach, was selected for the driveway, with grass joints to give it a more garden-like appearance. The utility parking areas to the north and south of the main drive are of tabby concrete, a concrete with seashells added to the surface, installed by Connery Concrete.

Two different species of Ficus *form an arch over the drive of coral stone, with* Zoysia *grass joints. At the house,* Ptychosperma macarthurii *palms are underplanted with a low hedge of* Carmona microphylla *and* Tabernaemontana divaricata *"Flore Pleno" against the walls.*

LAKESIDE GARDEN

First on our order of business in the Lakeside Garden was to remove all the existing grade changes. We wanted to design a garden without the steep declines between loggia and garden that made it so uncomfortable. The pool, steps, and paving were removed, and fill dirt was brought in to bring the level of the garden to just one comfortable step below the finished elevation of the rear loggia. The new relationship allowed a much more gracious transition between house and garden, and—although it was done for comfort—the leveling of the garden also made it feel larger.

The Lakeside Garden is centered on the view from the loggia to the waterway. In the middle is a large fountain, a focal point, carved from limestone that looks similar to the coral stone used for the paving, but is much more robust. The harder stone was necessary if we were to avoid the erosion caused by the flowing water. The floor of the fountain basin is finished in the same encaustic tile as the house loggias, which helps to unify the different spaces of the garden. The terrace around the fountain is for small dinner parties and other similar gatherings, and can accommodate as many as four large tables. To provide seating in the fountain area when there is not an event, or if overflow seating is needed, the basin walls of the fountain are at bench height. Next to the fountain terrace, the two existing *allées* of royal palms were replicated with new, healthier specimens in order to maintain the historical appearance of the house when seen from the Lake Trail, as well as to provide shade in the central part of the garden.

A limestone fountain is surrounded by terra-cotta pots planted with seasonal flowers. It is flanked by Roystonia regia *palms, and* Bougainvillea *"New River" climbs the facade of the house.*

Above: A historic Ceiba pentandra *tree is underplanted with* Viola hederacea. *Beyond it,* Schefflera *"Amate" and* Caryota mitis *palms form a dense barrier at the property line.*

Left: A secret walkway of coral flagstones is bordered by tropical plants.

TWO POOLS

Just beyond the rows of royal palms are two long pools, one for wading and lounging, the other for koi and water plants. During construction, the clients decided to change the koi pool to a lap pool, but the change came early enough that it could be made with little effort. We were able to design the lap-pool system so that the koi pond can be resurrected in the future, if they wish. Although the two pools are slightly different, they look the same from the garden. Each has a coral-stone coping that is raised slightly above the lawn, and an encaustic water-line tile.

Collaborating with Deborah, Chuck, and Jackie, we sited the pool cabana on the northern side of the wading pool, to take advantage of the windbreak the northern property-line buffer plants would provide in the winter months. This also allowed the cabana to be set among the Jurassic-looking kapok roots. There are sun terraces on each side of the cabana, and the one closest to the tree has a cut-out in the paving around one of the roots, giving the impression that the cabana and terraces have existed long enough for the tree to grow through the paving. Again, repeating materials to create continuity in the garden, the terraces next to and under the cabana are of coral stone (on the outside of the structure) and encaustic tile (under the roof).

Between the cabana and the property line, a collection of tropical plants provides an attractive backdrop. This multilayered arrangement of *Heliconia*, gingers, palms, tree ferns, and several varieties of shrub creates a dense buffer, blocking views of the neighboring property. To create symmetry, and to add more planting, we mirrored this tropical buffer on the other side of the garden, although the plant selection was different. Here, a tall *Ficus* hedge provided all the screening we needed, so we made this plant border narrower, allowing us to add a path, and did not limit ourselves to plants with dense foliage. We selected citrus trees and repeated them along the buffer. Around them, we added a wide variety of flowering and foliage plants. The path, of coral flagstone with grass joints, allows entry to the interior of the buffer and provides a private setting to enjoy the varied specimens; it also allows easy access for cutting flowers and foliage for the house. The rear pathway runs the length of the property, connecting the loggia to the rear property line.

The massive roots of the Ceiba pentandra *tree come very close to the pool pavilion.*

An allée of Roystonia regia *palms frames the limestone fountain and central facade of the house. The lawn of* Zoysia *grass extends from the coral-stone terrace to the two pools.*

LAKE TRAIL ACCESS

Hidden from view at the far end of the garden, a set of gentle coral ramp steps with rounded risers leads to a small terrace about 4 feet below the level of the main garden, and almost invisible from the house. It provides access to the Lake Trail and boat docks. The gentle slope and rounded risers allow items to be transported more easily, and are much more comfortable to walk up than are traditional steps. Decorative terra-cotta pots are displayed on shelves in the walls, and the ornate built-in bench is covered in antique encaustic tile. Between the terrace and the Lake Trail itself, we designed a metal gate based on the original ironwork found on the house.

Opposite, top: Conocarpus erectus *borders the Lake Trail, with* Bougainvillea *'New River" above it at garden level. A hedge of* Podocarpus macrophyllus *against the retaining wall creates a buffer that blocks views from the Lake Trail into the garden.*

Opposite, bottom: The landing at the foot of the ramped steps is seen from the Lake Trail. The pots are planted with drought-tolerant Graptopetalum paraguayense.

Right: The base of the kapok tree looms behind the pool and its pavilion.

MAUTNER GARDEN

Claudia Visconti Clippinger, Senior Associate

Owen McGoldrick, Photographer

Opposing tastes and contrasting desires can provide an unexpected opportunity for a unique project. The title of our first book, *The Civilized Jungle* (2009), embodied the joining of differing styles and alluded to the way harmony can be found even among dissimilarity. This is displayed artfully at the garden of Hans and Victoria Mautner in Jupiter Island, Florida. Hans wanted a wild, tropical garden, while Victoria envisioned clipped hedges and open lawn. We therefore had to develop a scheme that was both formal and informal, with a seamless yet obvious transition between the two. We created garden rooms using perimeter hedges to house the different styles, side by side, yet separate. Breaches in the hedges allow the spaces to flow, and evoke a sense of mystery as one passes through each. The result is a tropical yet well-trimmed paradise that appeals to both tastes.

1. MOTOR COURT AND FRONT GARDEN
2. MIDDLE GARDEN
3. HER GARDEN
4. HIS GARDEN
5. JUNGLE GARDEN

The gate columns leading out of Her Garden are covered with Ficus repens. *The tall hedge is of* Podocarpus macrophyllus, *and the* Brugmansia *tree drops its elegant white, yellow, and orange blooms onto the grass.*

Tall hedges of Podocarpus macrophyllus define the Front Garden. On the facade of the house is Bougainvillea *"New River," and* Brugmansia *trees frame the fountain.*

MOTOR COURT AND FRONT GARDEN

This site, on a corner lot, enticed us to design the Motor Court off axis with the main entry, and put it to one side of the house instead. It is lined with *Podocarpus macrophyllus* hedges along the roadside, and two spherical bollards flank the driveway apron to reinforce this skewed access point. Just in front of the hedges is a pair of large *Ficus* (fig) trees brought from elsewhere on the site. Swaths of *Anthurium* fill the understory of the figs and give color to the entrance. Bricks laid on their sides edge an infill of flat, aged brick arranged in a solider course pattern. The house behind is covered with *Bougainvillea* "New River," to soften the court and bring the architecture into the garden right away. Framed by the hedge opening from the road, and head on as you pull in, is an antique limestone fountain with a raised basin and decorative lion spitter. A void between the two lower windows offered the perfect spot for this low wall fountain. *Brugmansia* trees on either side of the fountain are placed in front of the windows, so that their beautiful blooms are visible from outside and inside. To the west of the motor court, a service drive screened by hedges is entered through a different apron from the road.

The building turns north just after the fountain wall, creating the perfect niche for a garden room. Also bordered by *Podocarpus* hedges, and further enclosed by a single black gate, this space is not visible from the Motor Court. Beyond the gate a short path leads to a potager, complete with herbs and flowers for a beautiful kitchen garden. In the center of the planting beds sits a large pot filled with annuals, a pleasant resting spot for the eye among the geometric beds and loose perennial border.

A double black gate to the east of the Motor Court opens to the house's entry path. Again, skewing the axis of the main entry to the house, a long, rectangular planter terminates the first leg of this path. The planter is filled with annuals that catch the eye, luring the visitor into pausing here before finally finding themselves on axis with the front door. An *allée* of *Ptychosperma elegans* (Alexander palms) lines the path leading to a pair of gardenias against the facade of the house. This part of the building is also covered in bougainvillea, rendering the house secondary to the garden.

*Night-blooming jasmine (*Cestrum nocturnum*) is trained on the wall of the house. The parterre beds are bordered with brick and separated by gravel paths, and a sphere of* Eugenia *sits in a vase d'Anduze in the center.*

MIDDLE GARDEN

The stairs that lead into the Middle Garden from the loggia are off-center with the garden space, owing to the architecture of the house, but we designed the garden to feel as though all is on axis. Large white stone urns line the ends of the three steps, matching the stone of the columns; they contain annuals, which are changed seasonally. (At SMI we do our best to keep the maintenance cost of annuals low, and one way to do that is to contain them in pots for an easy switch-out each season.)

This garden room is the thread that stitches together the two garden styles requested by Victoria and Hans. We originally designed it as a large checkerboard terrace, but the couple decided to leave it as a grassed open space. Four Medjool date palms (*Phoenix dactylifera*) define the corners, their generous fronds offering light shade overhead. Beyond the grass is an undulating border of perennials with a central bed of *Bambusa vulgaris* "Vittata" (golden Hawaiian bamboo), underplanted with *Monstera deliciosa*. At the bend of the undulation, a pair of stone pots planted with *Ruellia* adds a beautiful touch of purple. The beds are lined with *Carmona* to give them a clipped, contained finish.

The entire site is lined with tall hedges of *Podocarpus macrophyllus*, visible at the very back of this garden room. These hedges continue as the divider of this space from the two garden rooms on either side of it. These two gardens—Her Garden and His Garden—are formal and informal respectively, so the Middle Garden plays an important role in creating cohesion throughout the site. To make the transition among the three gardens more seamless, there are no gates in the gaps in the hedges; instead, the openings offer a vista through the spaces, giving depth and creating a sense of mystery about what is beyond. Small stone finials on the ground at each opening reinforce the start of each new room and provide visual rhythm down the axis.

The golden stems of Bambusa vulgaris *"Vittata" (golden Hawaiian bamboo) glow in front of the* Podocarpus macrophyllus *hedge. They are underplanted with* Monstera deliciosa, *and the stone urns are filled with purple-flowering* Ruellia.

HER GARDEN

West of the Middle Garden are a broken stone path and an elegant pool that terminates in a small terrace. Two planters filled with annuals line the entrance. This garden room is closely trimmed and well-kept, and appears formal. As a contrast to this tidy space, tall specimens of the palm *Areca catechu* on the far western property line, beyond the pool terrace, screen views of and from the adjacent property. A 6-foot-tall hedge of orange jasmine (*Murraya paniculata*) bounds the garden room, creating a green "wall" over which the palms peer.

At the back corners of the swimming pool sit two stone lions that separate the terrace from the pool coping, which otherwise appears continuous. Chaises longues and an umbrella-shaded table allow poolside relaxation and dining, and a white urn centered at the back of the terrace contrasts with the bright green of the hedge behind it. The urn provides a focal point across the pool, on axis with the entrance to this "room."

Access to the service drive is on the southern border of this space, and this is the entry point for the gardener, so the broken coral path continues from the terrace to prevent foot traffic from damaging the lawn. Patterned black double gates close off the service drive to give privacy for those in the garden, while avoiding a solid wall at the end of the path. A magnificent *Brugmansia* in the corner redirects the eye and softens the squareness of the space. For Victoria, this garden room is a retreat from the comparative chaos of her husband's jungle garden across the way.

HIS GARDEN

From the Middle Garden, a right turn leads east into a contrasting garden, where a pair of the Medjool date palms from the Middle Garden flank the opening to Hans's tropical paradise. Bermed sod creates an unusual lawn for the grove of coconut palms that fills this space. Some are planted at grade, while others sit atop the mounds. Patterns of shadow created as the sunlight hits their fronds make architectural art on the ground. This garden, too, is enclosed by *Podocarpus* hedges, allowing it to speak the same language as the other spaces. The trimmed, erect hedges are in sharp contrast with the staggered-height palms, and a large antique urn filled with white flowers is a focal point in the disorganized grid of palms. This urn is all that can be seen down the axis from the Middle Garden: The palms are screened by hedges at eye level, so that the space appears formal until it is entered and the tropical elements become apparent.

Coconut palms are planted in bermed sod, all framed with more tall hedges of Podocarpus macrophyllus.

JUNGLE GARDEN

To the south of His Garden is a disguised path that leads to the unseen, overgrown Jungle Garden. This garden contains a mix of shade plants that are shielded from the sun by palms and a gumbo-limbo tree (*Bursera simaruba*). Among these plants are tropicals as well as plants to attract butterflies. The plants are packed in so that the beds appear lush, in contrast with the tamed hedge behind them. A path of terrazzo aggregate leads to what was originally a grove of fruit trees. Valencia and navel oranges, ruby grapefruit, and lime trees once grew in a triangulated layout along the undulating walkway. These trees have since been removed because of citrus disease problems in Florida, and replaced with magnolias. Green areas among the trees allow space for outdoor entertainment. There is a strong contrast between the tight, heavily vegetated portion of the path and the grove of trees, from where the lawn opens up to the front of the house once more. When looking from the entry back to the lawn, the openness of the space allows it to look more expansive, adding to the drama of the entry. Mystery, or, as the Japanese call it, *yugen*, is crucial in garden design. Creating spaces and paths that surprise the visitor and trick the eye gives character and interest to a garden.

NASON GARDEN

Brian Vertesch, Senior Associate

Roger Foley, Photographer

Working with Dana and Quentin Nason, we developed what became a tropical oasis in Coral Gables. Living most of the time in England, which is surely the gardening capital of the world, this young couple were no strangers to designed gardens, and were familiar with and admiring of many of the English gardens that we brought up in conversation. However, they made a point of letting us know that when they visit Florida, they want to feel as if they are in the tropics and not in the English countryside.

On our first visit to the property we found an overgrown jungle, hiding what appeared to have been an attractive house at one time. The vegetation was so thick that you could not see more than 5 feet in any direction. The grounds also contained several abandoned fountain basins that had become successful hatcheries for amphibians and mosquitoes. After spending some time in the almost impenetrable bush, we managed to find and catalog a good number of trees and palms that we could use in the renovation.

We also toured the house, garage, and guesthouse with the architect, Rafael Portuondo of Portuondo Perotti Architects. He explained the historical significance of the house, as well as the substantial renovations that he would undertake to bring it back to life. Of particular interest to SMI were the addition of a garden room and loggia to the main house, and the garage renovation, which would include a pool cabana that would extend into the garden.

The property is fairly substantial for that part of Coral Gables, and we wanted to accentuate that size. The different "rooms" would need to incorporate tropical planting, as well as hardscaping that was native to the tropics, and preferably local or traditional to this area in particular. Privacy was also important, since the house is on a busy road.

Throughout the project the collaboration between SMI, the client, and the architect was enjoyable and fruitful. The connections between the house and garden developed to feel very natural and fluid. We at SMI—as well as Dana and Quentin, who loved it—felt that we had created a garden they could discuss proudly with aficionados on either side of the Atlantic.

1 ENTRY GARDEN AND PARTERRE
2 FAMILY GARDEN
3 SWIMMING POOL
4 PARKING COURT

Reclaimed encaustic floor tile and custom-made cast-stone wall sconces give the new loggia a feeling of history.

ENTRY GARDEN AND PARTERRE

The renovations to the front of the house revealed an attractive facade, but also exposed the living room to the busy right of way outside the three sets of French doors. In order to shelter the family from intrusive views, a hedge of *Podocarpus* was used to create a small private garden just outside the living room.

This was the only place where we brought in a little of the formal parterres of some English gardens. The parterre contains shrubs of two different colors, dark green and silver, in a simple design that reflects and pays homage to the work of the garden designer Russell Page (1906–1985) in Italy, at the Villa Silvio Pellico, Turin. In the middle of the parterre, large terra-cotta pots act as accents, planted with a mix of tropical flowers. The pots provide interest from the interior rooms, and can be seen from the front entry walk, too.

Just beyond the hedge, between it and the sidewalk, a pair of flowering *Solanum wrightii* trees further screen the house from the street, as well as providing depth to the garden when it is seen from the house. The hedge and trees provide the necessary screening at a human level, but allow views of the sky and canopy. Several large mahogany trees in the median strip outside the house create a borrowed view that makes the property seem more expansive. Purple bougainvillea trained on the wall of the house provides an explosion of color against the white facade. As well as making it accessible from the house, we added two gates from this space, one to the garden behind the house and one to the main entry walk.

The main access to the house is a simple curved walkway of coral stone, which reflects the residential nature of the neighborhood and is typical of houses of this age. The simple planting that lines it consists of flowering gardenia shrubs. Using the traditional coral, but straying from a traditional layout, we implemented a driveway that the client felt would provide a softer look to the front entry area and gardens. The coral stones are separated with grass joints, and between the two ribbons for the car tires is a wider strip of grass. The drive leads to the renovated porte cochère, where the surface becomes solid once more. Under the porte cochère, and continuing to the garage, we worked with Jim Connery of Connery Concrete to develop just the right color of tabby concrete, a product Jim has mastered, made with seashells added to the surface. A coral-stone border was added to the tabby to add further continuity of materials in the garden.

Opposite: Coral stone with strips of Zoysia *grass creates a softer driveway.* Buxus microphylla *var.* japonica *and* Gardenia jasminoides *"Miami Supreme" line the walkway.* Podocarpus macrophyllus *hedges and* Bougainvillea *"New River" can be seen in the background, and on the right is a* Solanum wrightii *tree underplanted with* Begonia *"Odorata Alba."*

Right: In the parterre, formal plantings of Podocarpus macrophyllus *"Pringles" and silver-leaved* Conocarpus erectus *var.* sereceus *surround large terra-cotta pots planted with seasonal flowers. A decorative metal gate separates the entry garden from the family garden beyond.*

FAMILY GARDEN

Once visitors pass through the gate into the Family Garden, they are led along a coral flagstone path past tropical fruiting trees to the new pool cabana. In addition to the gate at the parking area, access to this garden is also possible from the front parterre garden and the house, via the loggia. On entering, visitors experience vast open views, in contrast to the tighter Parterre and Parking Court. This was a conscious design decision: When designing the circulation for many of our projects, we incorporate compression and expansion, as well as the play of light and shade, in the progression.

The expansive Family Garden takes up almost half of the property, and its elements were arranged to accentuate the size of the grounds. Its main axis runs south–north from the road at the front all the way to the property line at the back. A secondary axis runs east–west, from the Parking Court gate to the eastern property line.

The lawn throughout the Family Garden is of *Zoysia*, which forms a smooth, hard surface that can accept most lawn furniture. In limiting the amount of paving in the pool area, and using the *Zoysia* continuously instead, the Family Garden looks much larger than if it were divided with paving. The lack of paving also gives a much softer look, and reduces glare, and the *Zoysia* forms a green carpet that ties the space together.

At the opposite end of the long axis from the pool, the garden is much less formal and more relaxed. We moved several royal palms (*Roystonia regia*) from elsewhere on the property to form a small grove, and placed a collection of rustic furniture—another of Dana's acquisitions from England—to act as the focal point at this end of the garden. Around the lawn, a collection of plants provides the lush tropical feeling that our clients wanted to experience when they escape England.

A new loggia extending from the house into the Family Garden forms the perfect vantage point. Its floor is of antique encaustic tile with a coral-stone border. The encaustic tile is made of concrete, and although this type originated in Europe, forms are commonly found in older buildings throughout the Caribbean. From the loggia, the pool and rustic furniture, along with other elements, such as a small antique sculpture and a birdbath, draw the eye deeper into the garden and allow one to take notice of the tropical foliage in varying sizes and textures.

SWIMMING POOL

We placed the swimming pool to terminate the view at the northern end of the long axis of the Family Garden, lined up with the cabana. Since pools are not used most of the time, we design many to act as fountains, and this one is no exception. To maintain a sense of history, as elsewhere in the garden, coral stone was used for the coping and walls of the pool, and also clads the three fountain pilasters that rise from the water. Small lead medallions cover the water source on each pilaster. Italian terra-cotta pots planted with false agave act as additional accents on top of each pilaster. Between the pilasters, coral-stone benches below the water level allow swimmers to relax and take in the long view across the garden to the front of the property. The floor of the pool is a very simple cobalt-blue tile—another material traditional to the age of the house. Although it is intense in color, when viewed from further into

the garden it complements the coral stone and lawn very well, and the pool becomes a jewel in a sea of green.

At the end of the pool, opposite the cabana, a large antique column base and urn that Dana found in London were placed as a focal point and planted with flowers. Behind the pool, existing clusters of *Ravenala madagascariensis* (traveler's palm) form a backdrop to the urn and also help to screen the property line. On the wall behind the three fountain pilasters, purple bougainvillea gives the terminus of this view even more punch. The only solid deck for the pool area is a simple coral-stone terrace between the cabana and the pool itself.

PARKING COURT

At the end of the driveway are the garage and guesthouse. The renovations to the garage included giving up some square footage for parking in favor of the new pool cabana, so extra off-street parking was needed for family and guests. Studying where to place it, we decided that using the area nearest the garage would leave the most space for the gardens. However, we also realized that this spot was visible from the kitchen and guesthouse, so we would need to come up with a solution that was sensitive to these views. The plan that developed was to create what would look like an informal garden terrace of coral flagstone with sod joints. Four bridal veil trees (*Caesalpinia granadillo*) were added to provide dappled shade that would keep the area and any vehicles cool, as well as contributing to the atmosphere we wanted to create.

Tall *Podocarpus* hedges form a green wall that separates the Parking Court from the pool garden beyond, and define the space. The hedge is pierced by a large gate that blocks views of the lower level, where vehicles may be parked, while allowing views of the more attractive elements beyond through a small ornamental opening. When devoid of cars, as it usually is, the Parking Court looks more like a space for functions—perhaps awaiting cafe tables and other furniture—than for the parking of automobiles.

Coral flagstones lead from the pool cabana to a decorative gate separating the Parking Court from the Family Garden. Ravenala madagascariensis *palms,* Heliconia, Alocasia odora *"California," and* Begonia *"Odorata Alba" create a barrier on either side of the gate.*

In the new loggia, the dining table is accentuated with a cut branch from one of the Solanum wrightii trees in the Entry Garden.

PATTERSON GARDEN

Claudia Visconti Clippinger, Senior Associate

Owen McGoldrick, Photographer

Susan and James Patterson approached us when they were looking to purchase a Landmark house in Palm Beach. The house was designed by Addison Mizner in the mid-1920s, and the Pattersons wanted to make sure that the beauty of the original architecture was not lost during the reconstruction. They hired the local architect Mark Marsh to spearhead the restoration of the house, and Mark, with whom we have worked on many occasions, recommended SMI. The property, on South Ocean Boulevard, has the advantage of expansive sea views. But when we first saw it, the lawn was at the same height as the road, which meant that the view was solely of passing cars and asphalt. We knew immediately that the site had much more potential. With open minds, the Pattersons allowed us to propose what we felt would be the ideal scenario for this property.

During the schematic phase of any project, our approach is to suggest the form and function of the overall site. There are no details in the schematic drawing; no paving materials or plant species. In this initial phase, our goal is to capture the essence of the client's desires by putting this on paper in a fashion that speaks to them aesthetically and functionally. Learning about a client and translating what you know into a new garden is one of the most enjoyable and challenging parts of the design process. Having learned that Susan was a champion swimmer, for example, we made the dimensions and placement of a competition-size pool dictate the layout of the garden. Capitalizing on the property's elevation changes, we also placed great importance on sunken and raised gardens to direct the form further. The gardens are now entirely personalized to the clients' way of life—a true success for us.

1. MOTOR COURT
2. FRONT LAWN
3. WEST TERRACE
4. LOWER GARDEN

*Florida flame vine (*Pyrostegia venusta*) grows on the pergola, below which is* Begonia *"Odorata Alba"; a pair of citrus are underplanted with baby sun rose (*Aptenia cordifolia*).*

Below: Richly stained pecky cypress "porton" gates lead off the main drive.

Opposite: Hedges of Ficus microcarpa *"Green Island" create green garden walls on either side of another cypress gate.*

MOTOR COURT

We wanted to create a sense of entrance—a feature that the existing driveway lacked, making the estate seem distant and uninviting. With a side entrance as the front door and a narrow space between the main house and the guest wing, we decided to place the Motor Court in front of the house. Allowing the architecture and site to determine the form of the driveway, we designed a circle off-center from the axis that runs to the front door. As a result, there is no interference with the front garden, and, with the driveway kept to the side, there is a feeling of arrival. In the limited area we wanted to use, the circle design allowed ample turnaround and drop-off room, but remained secondary.

The driveway is of recycled brick, broken up by bands of Dominican coral. In the center of the circle a collection of *Pandanus utilis* (screw pine) creates a domed effect. The central pine has a single trunk and is the tallest of the group, acting as the peak of the dome; those that surround it are multistemmed and a little shorter. The landscape just outside of the circle was kept to a minimum, mostly grass and small areas of *Ficus microcarpa* "Green Island," in order to keep this space low-maintenance and enhance the scale of the circle.

Continuing west, one can drive past the front door and pass through a "porton." The scale of the gates adds to the effect of the estate entrance. Just before the "porton," a guest garden bounded by a hedge of *Rhaphiolepis indica* (Indian hawthorn) lines the southern side of the driveway. A cloister breezeway offers windows into this garden space as you drive by. Since it is perpendicular to the guesthouse, one is led to this garden by coral paths. Low walls screened by taller hedging enclose this space and allow it to feel private while still offering public views from the driveway. Guests can spend time on the central terrace, listening to the white noise of the fountain. This fountain was already on the property, and we revitalized it using artisan-made tiles. Pots of cacti line the tiered steps of the fountain walls.

Beyond the gates is a large service drive in asphalt bordered with brick. *Clusia* was planted on either side of the eastern recreation wall to act as an extension of this screening. Norfolk pines behind the wall give height and screening on the opposite side. Through a breach to the north, a broken coral path leads to the swimming pool and surrounding garden. This path is mostly used by the gardeners and for service.

FRONT LAWN

Entering the house and turning eastward, guests reach the front lawn from the loggia onto a Dominican coral terrace. When the Pattersons bought the property, this lawn was at an almost equal elevation with the road, which meant the beautiful ocean just across the street was invisible. Immediately, we knew the lawn must be raised. Elevating it by about 4½ feet required the addition of a 7-foot-high retaining wall on the northern, southern, and eastern borders. This wall is screened with a hedge of *Ficus microcarpa* "Green Island." Owing to the salt spray and strong breeze from the ocean, it was necessary to use a very hardy plant. The Green Island ficus was contract-grown in order to have a 4-foot hedge at the time of installation, and it has since grown to the full height of the wall. Beyond, a change to Indian hawthorn around the curved corner of the wall gives way once more to Green Island ficus, giving a clean look from the Motor Court. On this side, Dominican coral steps lead to a pecky cypress gate that accesses the large, open lawn, which is lush and green. *Zoysia* "Cashmere" was chosen to give a true "green carpet" look to the space. The view of the water is now uninterrupted, and cars pass below the height of the wall, invisible from the garden.

On the interior side of the wall, Green Island ficus was also planted as screening, since a hardy, salt-tolerant plant was needed there, too. To keep this portion of the garden open, the planting is restricted to the perimeter. Coconut palms of varying height line the northern border, and beyond them is a large *Coccoloba uvifera* (seagrape tree), moved from elsewhere on the site. Additional seagrapes were collected and planted here to create more dense screening to the neighboring house. *Araucaria heterophylla* (Norfolk Island pines) along the western side provide a strong but elegant contrast to the palms.

*The open lawn is of Zoysia "Cashmere"; coconut palms contrast with Norfolk Island pines on the west side, and seagrape trees (*Coccoloba uvifera*) are planted on the north side.* Ficus microcarpa *"Green Island" lines the eastern border.*

WEST TERRACE

From the lawn, a pair of stucco columns adorned with Dominican coral caps mark a walkway onto the West Terrace. This portion of the terrace gives access down to the Lower Garden or onward to the larger terrace. To the northwest of the West Terrace is a more open terrace, and the two are joined by the loggia. Using the same materials as the front terrace has allowed the two spaces to appear as an extension of each other. The flat pebbles are laid in a much more intricate pattern on this side. A series of diamonds with large bands of circles frame the central part of the space, giving it a sense of division. We have found that deceiving the eye with a change in materials is a great tool for breaking up large spaces yet allowing them to flow.

Two *Tabebuia argentea* trees, underplanted with *Trachelospermum asiaticum* (jasmine minima), are the focal point of this space. The small beds in which they are set echoes the circular pattern of the pebbles. Stucco columns with a stepped brick base and Dominican coral caps with decorative wrought-iron rails tie in the terrace to the Lower Garden, and the transparency of the wrought iron allowed us to maintain views down to it. Blue-green vases d'Anduze are placed rhythmically along the rail and bordering facade, planted with *Ficus lyrata* (fiddleleaf fig) and *Clusia*. A lot of color has been introduced throughout this garden using glazed pots, and chaises longues and a small dining table make this lovely terrace suitable for many uses.

Yellow-blooming Tabebuia argentea *trees are underplanted with* Trachelospermum asiaticum*, and Vanda orchids hang from their branches; potted fiddleleaf figs (*Ficus lyrata*) stand by the railings.*

Citrus trees are underplanted with Trachelospermum asiaticum, *and* Ficus repens *covers the stair wall, underplanted with* F. microcarpa *"Green Island" and ground cover of the vivid* Tradescantia pallida *"Purpurea."*

LOWER GARDEN

Ramped steps lead down from the West Terrace to the Lower Garden, just after the step up from the front lawn to the terrace. This transitional point allows many axes and garden spaces to converge, and each space entices the visitor to take their next steps in that direction. At the bottom of the ramped steps the broken coral path continues to the small terrace at the far end of the swimming pool. Or you can continue straight to a break in the Green Island ficus hedge, which steps up to a slightly raised terrace.

Tucked into this space, so as not to interrupt the more visible garden rooms, is a spa on an axis with the swimming pool. It is frequently the case that spas are not used as much as the client may envision, so we disguise them in our gardens to act as water features rather than only a jacuzzi. Often it is simply a jet of water from the center that can transform a spa into a fountain. Gracing the western side of this water feature is a classical stone bench, which offers one of the best views of the garden, allowing an axial view down the swimming pool to a blue-and-white azulejo wall fountain in the wall of the West Terrace. A scalloped coquina shell fills with water and gently drops water into the pool. Engaging the swimming pool with a fountain is another tool we use to blend a recreational water feature with the surrounding garden, so as not to detract from its beauty.

The swimming pool is an Olympic-sized lap pool, so that Susan can enjoy her daily exercise. Its elongated shape provides a strong axis feature for the rear garden as a whole. To keep the length of the pool to a minimum, stairs lead off to each side in a half-moon shape, extending from the rectangular geometry. A pair of cobalt-blue vases d'Anduze sit on the ledge on each side of the stairs, further incorporating the pool into the garden. It is lined with coral coping bordered by pebbles laid flat, as in other parts of the garden. This cohesive use of materials creates a language for the entire garden that is altered in pattern and geometry to give visual interest and separation.

At the western end of the pool, an open terrace provides the opportunity for chaises longues and other poolside seating. The blue furnishings throughout the garden complement the blues of the tiles and ceramic vases.

Beyond the pool coping, an open lawn is planted with four citrus trees, each with a bed of jasmine minima below. While the wall fountain remains exposed, the rest of the wall is screened with bougainvillea, giving a soft backdrop from across the swimming pool. A low *Carmona* hedge and looser, colorful plantings at the bottom of the wall create layers and give depth, further nestling the wall into the landscape.

The two yellow-flowered Tabebuia argentea *are impressive on the raised terrace. By the pool are potted annuals in vases d'Anduze, and the walls are covered with* Bougainvillea *"New River," underplanted with* Ficus microcarpa *"Green Island" and* Tradescantia pallida *"Purpurea." Blue-and-white azulejo tiles border the shell fountain.*

PETERFFY GARDEN

Brian Vertesch, Senior Associate

Owen McGoldrick, Photographer

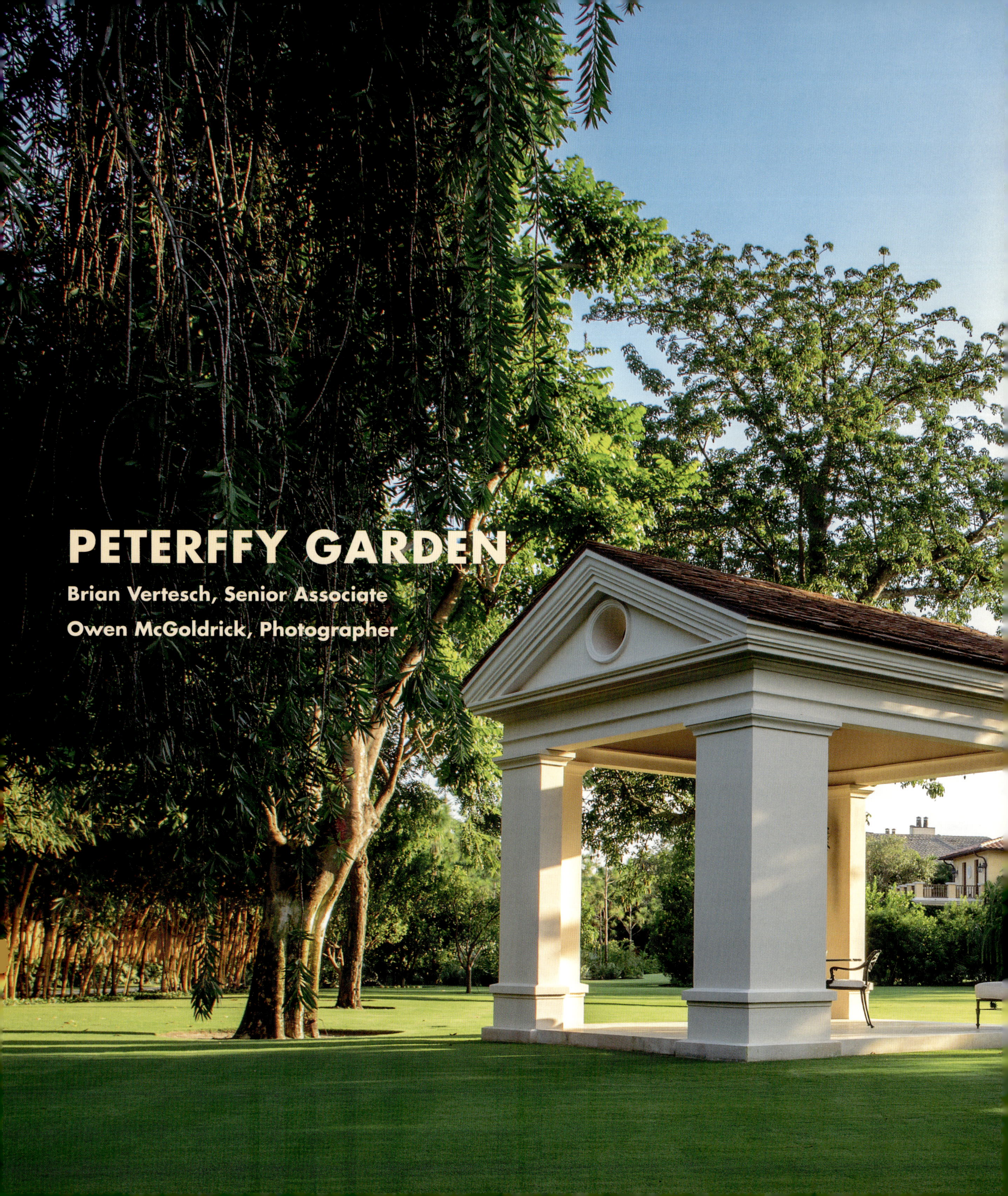

The Peterffy Garden occupies a large, irregularly shaped piece of land just south of the middle of Palm Beach. The lot was vacant for many years, and so, hoping to make it more attractive to prospective buyers by giving it more character, the owner planted several rows of citrus trees. The trees were visible from the road, and, although a folly, they led to the property becoming known to many local residents as "The Orange Grove." In the early days of our work on the site, people who heard we were working on the gardens for a new house worried more about what was happening to the citrus trees than about anything else.

The lot has an extremely long border with the Intracoastal Waterway. One third of the property is occupied by a mature mangrove forest and the rest contains several large trees. Two of the trees—a large baobab (*Adansonia*) and a canoe tree (*Cavanillesia platanifolia*)—had been designated Historical Specimen Trees by the Town. The trunk of the baobab, a native of Madagascar, is about 15 feet across (it can grow to more than 50 feet), and the tree stands about 70 feet tall. The canoe tree stood about 120 feet tall, and it had no branches below about 90 feet up the trunk. During Hurricane Irma in 2017, both trees were blown down; the baobab was able to be righted, but unfortunately the canoe tree could not be saved.

SMI's involvement with the garden started when the architect Dan Kahan invited us to collaborate on the project with his client, Thomas Peterffy. Our first task was to work with Dan to decide the proper placement of the house on the site. He explained the layout of the house and also expressed ideas he had related to placing it so that the main view over the water would be between two islands in the middle of the waterway. We thought this was an excellent idea, and after some study, we recommended pushing the house far to one end of the property in order to accentuate what is an abnormally long piece of land for Palm Beach. We also suggested that the entry gate for vehicles be placed at the far end of the property from the house, to create a long entry procession for visitors.

The concepts for the rest of the property revolve around giving the appearance that the house was built in the early days of Palm Beach and the gardens carved out of nature over time. Our client also expressed a love of walking through the garden and in nature, and asked for paths or other access so that he could stroll around and observe the progress of individual plants. Great care and study were also given to the relationship of the house with the adjacent waterway. Being able to collaborate with the client and architect from the beginning of the project—before the house had even been sited—allowed everyone involved to create an estate that took maximum advantage of what the land had to offer, including that much-loved orange grove.

1. ENTRANCE AND TROPICAL GARDEN
2. BAMBOO TUNNEL
3. MOTOR COURT
4. GREAT LAWN
5. MANGROVE FOREST
6. SWIMMING POOL GARDEN

The ceiling of the folly was left open to expose the terra-cotta roof tiles. Purple-flowering Vanda orchids are featured in the corner niches, and Bambusa vulgaris *"Vittata" can be seen beyond.*

ENTRANCE AND TROPICAL GARDEN

The main gate is about 450 feet from the house. This is extremely unusual for Palm Beach, since real estate is so valuable, but it allowed us to create an entry procession that passes through several different gardens before reaching the house. As the visitor progresses along the chain of spaces, glimpses of the house, gardens, waterway, and a folly are offered, making the sequence interesting while not revealing all the property has to offer.

After the large entry gates, the drive curves under and around an enormous banyan tree (*Ficus benghalensis*), with aerial roots that look like giant stalactites. Although there were detailed drawings for the driveway, the edge was placed on site to ensure that it passed the roots without requiring any pieces to be removed. This giant banyan, with two smaller *Ficus benjamina* trees next to it, provided the perfect canvas for a tropical garden.

Next to the drive and among the tree roots, layers of tropical plants create a jungle-like appearance. *Cyathea cooperi* (Australian tree fern), *Heliconia*, gingers, and bananas fill the space between the canopy of the trees and the ground, and the understory was filled with tropical begonias, bromeliads, *Peperomia*, *Alocasia*, and varieties of *Philodendron*. The mix of plants provides both flowering and textural interest as the various leaf sizes, shapes, and colors play off one another.

Keeping in mind our client's desire to explore the garden, we designed a small coral flagstone walkway that slips behind the banyan tree and leads to a bench in the middle of the Tropical Garden. The joints between the flagstones are of dwarf mondo grass rather than traditional mortar, to keep the garden as lush as possible.

BAMBOO TUNNEL

Against the wall that separates the tropical garden from the road outside, we placed *Bambusa vulgaris* "Vittata" (golden Hawaiian bamboo), which runs all the way along to the main motor court. The drive is very close to the front privacy wall here, leaving only enough space for the bamboo. We mirrored the placement of the bamboo on the other side of the drive, creating a cathedral-like vault that extends for almost 230 feet. To allow views of the house and adjacent gardens and to make sure that this section did not feel too enclosed, the foliage is removed from the stems up to a height of 7 feet. This also reveals the attractive yellow canes, which would otherwise be obscured by the leaves.

Right: Bambusa vulgaris *"Vittata," golden Hawaiian bamboo, creates a tunnel over the tabby seashell concrete drive.*

Opposite: Quercus virginiana *(live oak) trees frame the house, and columns of* Podocarpus macrophyllus *accentuate the facade. The coral-stone motor court is set slightly below the lawn of* Zoysia *grass.*

MOTOR COURT

At its far end, the shady Bamboo Tunnel opens onto a bright motor court, offering the first grand view of the house. Here, the planting palette changes to mostly native Florida plants that would have been typical to estates built in the early days of Palm Beach. Four live oak trees (*Quercus virginiana*) anchor the corners of the square court, framing the house. Coral-stone pavers are enclosed by a decorative raised curb in the same material, elevating the surrounding lawn, as though the Motor Court has been carved into the garden. A small circular planter in the middle of the court contains several *Guaiacum officinale* (lignum vitae) in a soft, pillow-like arrangement. The lawn is a lush, green carpet of *Zoysia* that ties the gardens together. Grass paths lead through arrangements of native shrubs, including stoppers (*Myricianthes fragrans*) and wax myrtle (*Myrica cerifera*), which screen views of the Motor Court from the Great Lawn beyond.

GREAT LAWN

As another way of accentuating the size of the property, we used the portion of land between the house, the Mangrove Forest, and the Tropical Garden at the entrance to create a large, open lawn. It is elliptical and slightly depressed in the middle, to create a bowl effect for extra character. The lawn extends from the client's office in the house to the end of the tropical garden. At the far end, opposite the office, we proposed a small folly to serve as a focal point and as a destination, to pull visitors farther into the garden. In collaboration with Dan Kahan, we developed the concept of a temple structure that would echo elements of the main building, but would be more rustic in its finishes. Dan also persuaded the Town's building department to allow the rustic roof structure, in which the tiles are exposed to the seating area below.

The lawn is ringed with specimen trees. We started by moving two existing specimen trees, which required an enormous crane and telephone poles to brace and support the trees after replanting. We then presented our client with images of and information about as many large trees that we felt were unique or rare to the area as possible. The trees he chose were arranged so as to present each one to its best advantage, while not creating problems with scale or unattractive color combinations. Under the trees we continued the concept from the Motor Court of using native plants, so that the edges of the garden look as though they are original to the island. The native *Serenoa repens* "Cinerea" (silver saw palmetto) is the dominant species in the border planting, which, as well as contributing to the historical appearance of the garden, also provides a natural-looking transition from the lawn to the Mangrove Forest beyond.

A small temple-like building was created as a folly and destination. The trunks of a Ceiba pentandra *and* Cavanillesia platanifolia *can be seen between it and the Mangrove Forest beyond.*

A large baobab, Adansonia digitata, *dominates the lawn of* Zoysia *grass.* Callistemon viminalis, Eucalyptus pauciflora, E. caliginosa, *and* Cocos nucifera *"Maypan" can all be seen in the distance.*

MANGROVE FOREST

At two points in the garden, where the Mangrove Forest meets the silver saw palmetto, visitors may catch a glimpse of a narrow boardwalk that leads from the Great Lawn into the forest. The idea of using the forest by creating a boardwalk materialized in our early meetings with the client, when we were discussing his love of walking in nature, and he quickly accepted it. Not only would the boardwalk create additional areas for our client to walk in the garden, but also it would allow us to activate a large portion of the grounds that had been considered off limits and unusable.

The boardwalk is 4 feet wide and is made of synthetic wood, with a simple, ribbon-like aluminum rail on one side. From it visitors can see crabs, raccoons, and fish among the stilt-like roots of the mangroves. It also extends out of the forest to the open waterway, where we created a small overlook. The landing was positioned in a part of the waterway that contains sea grasses, which require sunlight to grow—so we had to come up with a design that maintained our vision for an attractive gathering place. The design of the landing had to have openings that allowed sunlight to penetrate to the bottom of the waterway, and although we found several products that were specifically fabricated to allow light to penetrate, we found them all too industrial in appearance. We began developing our own teak version, based on the teak decks found on classic boats.

Once we had a concept, we made contact with a company that specializes in boat woodwork to help us to realize the design. Vern Mowrey, owner of the Yacht Shop in Newburyport, Massachusetts, provided great insight into the limitations and strengths of teak, and in the end he provided an exceptional product, which he says is the largest teak grate his firm has ever constructed. Although it is large compared to a boat deck, the platform is modest in size and simple in shape, and provides a comfortable setting for a small group to take a break before following the boardwalk back to the house and the Swimming Pool Garden.

An elevated boardwalk with a simple aluminum rail leads through the Mangrove Forest. It leads to a teak seating area made to allow light to penetrate through to the seagrasses underwater. Cocos nucifera *"Maypan" frame the view of the water across the lawn.*

SWIMMING POOL GARDEN

The simple Swimming Pool Garden focuses on views of the water, rather than drawing attention to elements of the garden. The dominant feature is the infinity pool, which appears to flow out into the adjacent waterway. If the infinity effect is to work well, the color of the pool water must be similar to that of the water into which it "flows." A challenge we faced here was that the color of the natural waterway changes often. We lined the pool with tile in a complementary blend of colors, and this has produced a successful effect, since the reflected color of the pool changes with varying environmental conditions just as the waterway does.

Between the house and the pool, we made a very simple terrace of coral stone with sod joints. The stones provide a firm surface, while the grass softens the terrace and reduces glare. Coconuts with curved trunks frame views of the water, and of the house when seen from a boat. On each side of the pool, a secret set of steps leads to a hidden lower terrace between the pool and the waterway, allowing direct access to the water's edge.

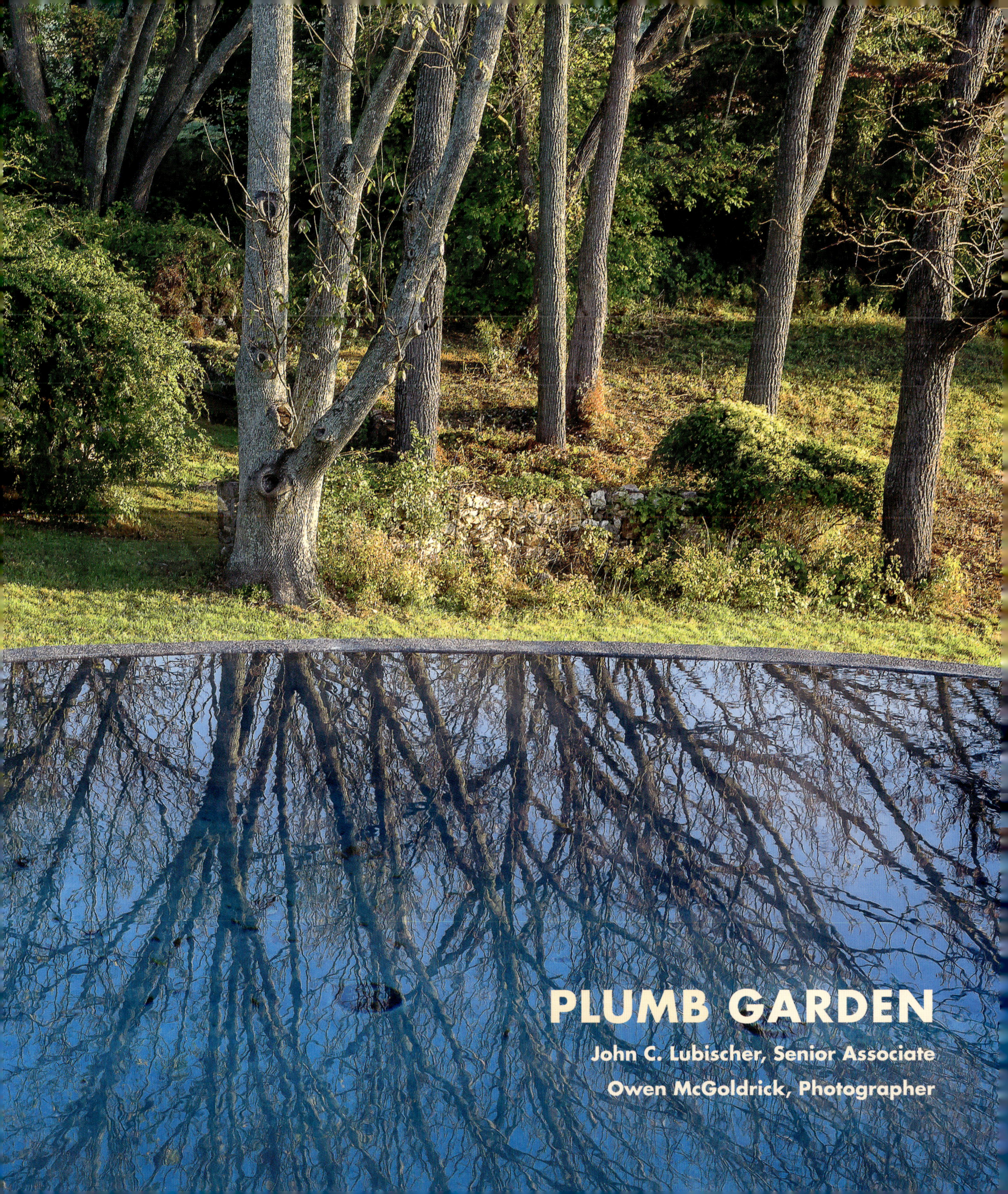

PLUMB GARDEN

John C. Lubischer, Senior Associate

Owen McGoldrick, Photographer

❶ ENTRANCE AND MOTOR COURT

❷ FRONT GARDEN

❸ TERRACES

❹ SWIMMING POOL

❺ GYM GARDEN

Cory and Matt Plumb became interested in SMI after we designed her sister's property in Coral Gables. The Plumbs' project was a remodeling of the Tea House, a country getaway in Chadds Ford, Pennsylvania, that had been expanded upon over the years. Wishing to recapture the original charm of the house, the couple commissioned SMI with the confidence that we could transform the grounds, not only aesthetically, but also in a way that would suit their family's needs and lifestyle.

Chadds Ford, with its country roads winding through hills and dales, is in one of the most scenic areas of the United States. That, coupled with the history of the area, dating back to Revolutionary times, and its fine public gardens, makes it a personal favorite of mine. The house and grounds that Cory and Matt created fit perfectly into their scenic surroundings, which is the best compliment one could give. The planting will grow and all will need care, but this garden is built to last.

ENTRANCE AND MOTOR COURT

The Plumbs wanted to keep the entrance low-key, and elected to do nothing to draw attention to it. From their unassuming gate, the drive up to the house is pleasingly long, with a soft incline. There are views of rolling fields on either side, the edges of old woodland, and a country road beyond. The main entrance runs around one side of an area of old oaks, maples, and a few towering pines. The wilds here are important in screening the house, adding mystery to the approach.

Lower than the woodland, an ample court runs parallel with the front of the Tea House and turns toward the woods. It is bordered with granite Belgian cobbles, which give an impression of permanence and contain the driving surface of the loose-laid, local grayish gravel.

Elevation changes throughout the grounds allowed the opportunity to create interest at nearly every turn, but sometimes they also posed problems. The Tea House is set low and the grounds directly in front drained toward it; the woodland beyond was the highest point. This meant that any motor court must be substantially lowered, for drainage. As the grade of the Motor Court was lowered, the elevation change at the woodland edge would need to be handled with a fairly tall retaining wall.

We created a handsome stacked-stone wall, with mortar that is held back, and seen only at the cap of the wall. Such walls are common in the area, and, when done well, create an instant impression of age and rustic countryside charm. The wall is irregular in appearance, with its variously sized stones and varied stacking. Images were presented by us and mock-ups of the wall were made by the installer, Lothar Ehrich of Ehrich & Ehrich Landscape Architects, to determine the range of stone size and the degree of looseness or tightness for the coursing. Of our clients, Cory was especially engaged in the selection process. She preferred a mid-sized to a large field stone, in a fairly loose or relaxed stack.

The wall is tallest in the middle, and graduates downward on both sides equally as it fans out. At the center, we designed an inviting set of steps that lead up into the old forest. The risers are made of stone and the treads grass. It is attractive and mysterious, drawing the visitor in to explore what lies beyond, and encouraging a stroll under the lofty canopy of the trees. It is our intention in the future that the woodland will be planted with ferns and ground cover of different textures, and white-flowering dogwoods of varying ages and sizes.

At the top of the Motor Court, between the Belgian block border and stone wall, we made a transition strip of grass about 5 feet wide. A couple of catch basins with no-nonsense cast-iron grates take rainwater away from the front of the house and the Motor Court. Here also we planted six Halka Shademaster honey locusts (*Gleditsia triacanthos* var. *inermis* 'Shademaster'). This tree is an SMI favorite for its flowing form and feathery leaves, and its canopy creates the most perfect dappled shade. The Plumbs felt the same.

Opposite: Enticing steps lead from the Motor Court into the old woodland.

Right: The original tea room section of the house is lined with a perennial bed and lead pots of annuals.

FRONT GARDEN

There are three entrances at the front of the house: the formal entrance to the Tea House; the mud-room entry, where most of the everyday activity of the house occurs; and the door that leads to the sitting room, office and bedrooms. The Motor Court closely approaches the formal front entry, and a short walkway of Pennsylvania bluestone leads to the front portico. A curved path of bluestone flagging set in mortar leads to the mud room, and a quaint, unassuming path of stepping stones cuts through the front lawn to the bedroom wing.

Along the front of the Tea House, we chose billowing hedges of the boxwood *Buxus* 'Green Mountain', and ended them with tall American boxwood trees, which were transplanted from elsewhere in the grounds. We placed a specimen saucer magnolia, *M.* x *soulangeana*, in front of the dining area, so that it can be seen from inside. Its growth habit is round and open; the bark is gray, and the tree has large, pale-pink flowers in early spring. Beyond it, we shielded views of the Motor Court with the tall boxwood. We planted ground cover of periwinkle (*Vinca*) beneath the magnolia, and added clematis to clamber through the tree. *Pyracantha* 'Mohave' (firethorn) is planted against the walls behind it, with a few compact *Prunus laurocerasus* 'Otto Luyken' (cherry laurel).

There is an array of evergreens against the bedroom wing of the house. These include more cherry laurel, *Pieris japonica* (Japanese andromeda), *Cephalotaxus harringtonia* and, as a featured accent, a large bird's-nest spruce (*Picea abies* 'Nidiformis'). A mature *Stewartia* tree was transplanted from elsewhere on the property, and strategically placed in the lawn to create depth and screen the bedrooms. Another transplant, a crape myrtle (*Lagerstroemia indica*), was placed to crowd the entrance of that wing slightly, so that it didn't feel open to the Motor Court. On either side of the door are dwarf Alberta spruces (*Picea glauca* var. *albertiana* 'Conica')—a plant that never fails to add charm.

A couple of lead urns were introduced as a detail, and also for annual color. They are set on old millstones that survived from the original estate.

The terrace overlooks the valley, with pond and pump house in the foreground.

TERRACES

Inside the Tea House, the great room or tea room leads off the foyer. From it, three sets of French doors open to the back of the house, to glorious views of rolling countryside. From its high vantage point the house overlooks a valley, a couple of ponds, rising wooded hills beyond, and hay fields that seem to go on forever.

This was a natural place to create a terrace where the Plumbs could entertain and enjoy the view. We began by leveling the slope with a stacked-stone retaining wall of Pennsylvania field stone, about 2 feet high. The terrace has a classic shape, along with a traditional treatment of stone with sod joints.

From this formal terrace, it is a comfortable walk on grass to the next one, off the dining room. It is made with bluestone and mortar joints, and has the same view of the countryside. It also overlooks a parterre garden of low boxwood hedges and herbs. A stacked-stone wall created the flat level necessary to contain the garden and handle the grade changes. Bluestone steps lead down to the lawn and toward the pool house. We planted a large thornless honey locust to bring some dappled shade to this terrace.

A wall of stacked Pennsylvania field stone holds the terrace, which has joints of New England bent grass. Climbing roses are trained against the Tea House.

SWIMMING POOL

The property already had an indoor pool, which had been added to the Tea House by the former owner. The Plumbs decided to demolish this portion of the house, along with the old pool. In the end they would have a freestanding pool house and an outdoor pool. With the Plumbs' approval, we decided to place the pool on the far side of the pool house. This was where the views were best of the valley and also a romantic ruin and a charming old stone pump house by a pond. We felt a negative-edge pool would produce the best effect, allowing water and view to meet. We made a built-in planter on either side of the pool entry and added two cut-leaf Japanese maples (*Acer palmatum* "Crimson Queen") to grace these spots.

The planter at the edge of the swimming pool contains Acer palmatum *"Crimson Queen"; the old pump house is behind.*

GYM GARDEN

Off the gym, in a small garden entered via steps of worn reclaimed granite, we made an arbor against an old brick wall. In the center of the garden, in an island of grass, we used a millstone as a plinth for a rustic urn; it is a place to add color with annuals. A collection of shade-loving hostas fills the beds, which have a northern exposure, and nestle beneath the arbor, along the brick wall. The hostas are a mix of varieties, from miniature to large, with leaves of green and silvery blue in various shades, some with white margins. Ground cover of periwinkle, *Pachysandra* and English ivy (*Hedera helix*) border the beds.

Below: Cephalotaxus harringtonia, *dwarf Alberta spruce (*Picea glauca *var.* albertiana *"Conica") and a perennial border of sedums and salvias.*

*Opposite: The Gym Garden with its hedge of American boxwood, arbor of pee gee hydrangea (*H. paniculata*) and central pot standing on a millstone.*

RAKOLTA GARDEN

John C. Lubischer, Senior Associate

Steven Brooke, Photographer

Terry and John Rakolta brought us in to rescue this project. Their new house on Everglades Island, Palm Beach, had been built, and the hardscape and landscapes were complete, yet they were not satisfied with it. After living with it for a while, Terry called SMI and explained her wishes. She felt exposed to the open bay and wanted privacy for herself and her family, and for guests, by eliminating views from boaters and other onlookers. She did not like the views from the garden, either. It is directly across the Intracoastal Waterway from a residential area in West Palm Beach, and, besides the views of those residences, she could also see the city high-rises to the north. The Rakoltas enjoyed all views of the water, but not those of city buildings. This was the challenge they presented to our team.

The Rakoltas and SMI could not be more pleased with the finished garden, which has been featured on the cover of *Garden Design Magazine* and in other publications, and has won many awards. The greatest reward for us, however, is the enjoyment it brings to the family and to all who visit.

1. MOTOR COURT AND COURTYARD
2. RUNNEL AND FOUNTAIN
3. POOL GARDEN
4. PALM ALLÉE

From the garden, arches of Ficus nitida *lead to Venetian steps beside the Intracoastal Waterway.*

MOTOR COURT AND COURTYARD

The Motor Court is secluded from the road, first by masonry walls and then by a hedge of *Ficus nitida*. The hedge continues in a graceful arch, bringing privacy from the street. We cut off the driveway to the service area and gave that space to the Courtyard instead.

From the Motor Court, a gate opens to a brick walk that first branches off toward the entrance of an enclosed courtyard garden. At its entrance is a large *Ficus benghalensis* (banyan) tree that brings shade and greenery. The Courtyard is floored with bricks in a large, classic diamond pattern with limestone banding. This is a protected space that the Rakoltas can use when the wind is blowing too strongly on the bay side. We greened the space with beds against the house, where large palm fronds and small potted palms create dappled shade. It is still a relatively sunny place, and Terry uses a red umbrella when the sun is overhead. The umbrella and furniture are gathered in front of the focal point of the courtyard, a walled Italianate, limestone water feature with coping that is wide enough to sit on.

A wrought-iron gate is flanked by a hedge of Podocarpus *and screening of* Ficus nitida. *At the entrance to the inner courtyard, a* Ficus *tree is festooned with bromeliads and orchids.*

In the inner courtyard, coquina and brick pattern terracing is edged with Adonidia *and* Rhapis *palms, with the large cut leaves of* Monstera deliciosa *in the foreground.*

RUNNEL AND FOUNTAIN

Off the library, in a narrow space shaded by *Ravenala madagascariensis* (traveler's palm) and *Dicksonia antarctica* (Australian tree fern), there is an exquisite antique limestone runnel and wall fountain. The sound of the water spilling into the runnel is very gentle and soothing to the ear. We planted the runnel on both sides with a dwarf *Spathiphyllum* (flowering ginger) and other tropical, textured plants.

A perfect garden path, with a soothing crunch beneath the feet. Terra-cotta pots are filled with the red ivy-leaved pelargoniums so characteristic of Italian gardens. The path leads to the arched entry of the pool loggia (opposite).

POOL GARDEN

From the pool loggia at the back of the house, Venetian-style steps lead down to the water. We separated this space with a colonnade of hedged arches on the south side of the pool to match that on the north side. This is reminiscent of the gardens of the Alhambra in Granada, Spain, where fountains play in "rooms" walled with arched hedges. Unlike in the Palm *Allée*, which we left open to the bay, here we added a pleached hedge of Ashoka trees (*Polyalthia longifolia*). It runs parallel to the bulkhead, and allows views of the waterway from both loggia and pool, while preventing boaters at a lower level than the bulkhead from seeing in. The fronds of the tall *Phoenix dactylifera* (Medjool date palms) to the north screen views of the city high-rises, but selectively: During the day they block out the undesirable building views completely, but at night the romantic reflections of the city lights can be seen. Mirrored lattices in two arches cut into the screening hedge on the northern property line create the illusion of another garden room.

The *Ficus* arches that line the southern side of the pool turn in a different direction, to run parallel to the water and the stepped bulkhead. They become windows to the water, giving a sense of privacy and defining the great lawn to the east. In the afternoon, as the sun sets, they cast shadows across the grass. These hedges were carefully made to be in proportion with the house, and they are in a rhythm that plays perfectly with the colonnade of the house. In this way one becomes an extension of the other. It is a practice of SMI to tie each garden to the house whenever possible.

East of the hedge, and running parallel to it, is a gravel path. Fine gravel, laid thinly on a well-compacted base with metal edging, makes the perfect garden path, with a soothing crunch beneath the feet. A low hedge planted along the path further defines the lawn. Large terra-cotta pots are set in front of the wall portion of each arch in the hedge, filled with the red ivy-leaf pelargoniums that are so characteristic of Italian gardens. The pots are a nice link to the barrel-tile railing of the second story of the house, and to the roof. *Bougainvillea* "New River" climbs up to the second floor of the house, where it gets the full sun that it loves. This, along with the green shutters, makes the house appear gardenesque. The gravel path continues to the southwestern seating area, from where the Venetian steps to the bay are fully visible.

A gravel path leads from the pool edge beyond the arches of Ficus nitida *with which the pool is lined. Opposite the loggia, a pleached hedge of* Polyalthia longifolia *(Ashoka tree) allows a glimpse of the Intracoastal Waterway beyond.*

PALM ALLÉE

A gate to the west of the Motor Court leads to an inviting *allée* of palms. Our choice for this spot was the silvery blue Medjool palm. With their architectural, ornamental trunks, the trees create interest from the ground right up into the high, cathedral-like canopy of fronds. Beneath, a gravel path is lined with *Ficus microcarpa* "Green Island." Together, path and palms direct the eye to a sculpture on a heavy stone pedestal, with the bay beyond. The view of the bay is deliberately narrowed by hedges that run perpendicular to it: the arched colonnade of tall *Ficus* to the south and a solid, tall hedge to the north.

LA SALONA

Claudia Visconti Clippinger, Senior Associate

Steven Brooke, Photographer

When the Beaux-Arts architect Marion Sims Wyeth designed this estate in Palm Beach, in 1926, the island was establishing itself as an affluent winter retreat. The architecture was influenced by European styles, and homes were being built as family estates for years to come. Wyeth was among the few first-generation Palm Beach architects who defined the town's vernacular. In 1929, another famous architect, the Swiss-born Maurice Fatio, designed an addition to this Mediterranean-style home, creating a larger living space and garden. The house was originally built for the Reynolds family, who founded First National Bank, and it was bought in the early 1980s by our client, Burke Ross.

Burke enlisted SMI's help at La Salona just a couple of years later. We replaced the gravel driveway with formal paving, removed some walls in the garden, and opened parts of the house to the outdoors. Burke wanted to respect the history of the house, so both it and the garden were redesigned to meet modern needs while reflecting the design principles of the past, making it into a home that could accommodate his family and give them a sense of privacy. Ample living space was the goal, and the garden was to play a strong part in that. Burke's love of gardens and his trust in our vision allowed us to be creative in the moving of walls in order to provide fluidity from interior to exterior. Neither of us knew that we were establishing a lifelong relationship and would continue to collaborate on the garden for many years.

1. MOTOR COURT
2. EAST LAWN
3. ATRIUM
4. SWIMMING POOL TERRACE AND COURTYARD
5. TROPICAL GARDEN
6. PRIVATE GARDEN

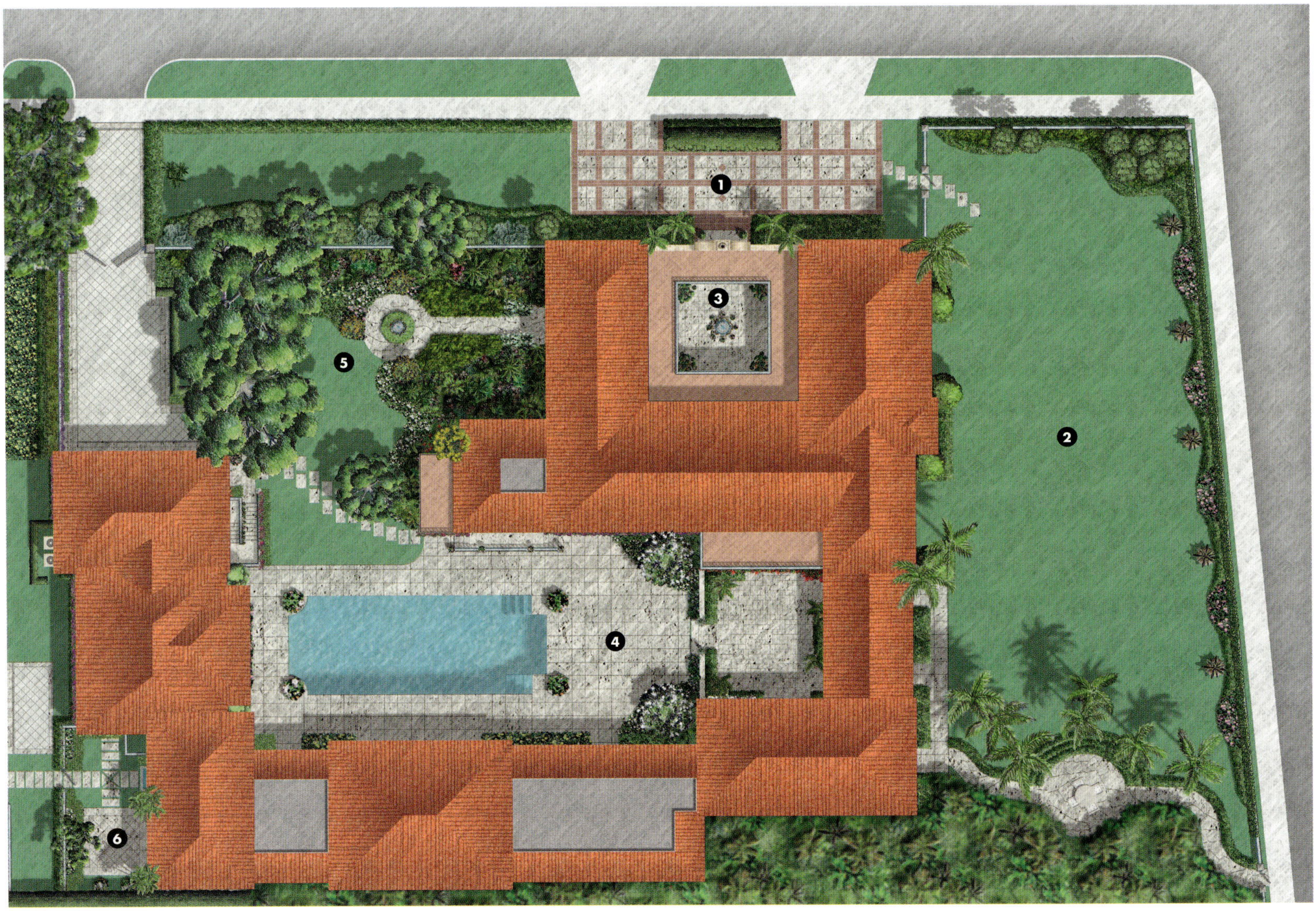

MOTOR COURT

The drive was originally gravel, and one of the first changes that Burke asked us to make was to create a solid-surface drive that would provide room for parking but not dominate the front entry. Respecting the architecture of the home, we designed a brick and coral drive in a grid, giving a sense of arrival but remaining secondary to the gorgeous architecture of the house. Simulated coral was used in order to reduce maintenance and extend the longevity of the driveway. Large pots containing *Garcinia spicata* flank the entry steps that lead to the original wooden estate doors.

Left: Thryallis *is planted against the house, with a border of Ganges primrose (*Asystasia gangetica*) and gumbo-limbo tree (*Bursera simaruba*). Across the lawn is a banyan tree, underplanted with* Monstera deliciosa.

Below: At the far side of the lawn, tall Sabal palmetto *is underplanted with* Ficus microcarpa, *with bump-outs of* Nerium oleander *"Ice Pink."*

EAST LAWN

From the Motor Court, stepping stones lead to the eastern garden gate, which opens to the oceanside lawn. This area is mainly open, with undulating planting at the perimeter. At the southern end, a coral walk from the house to the road has a raised gathering space for viewing the ocean. Tiers of *Ficus microcarpa* "Green Island" soften it and bring down the elevation of the gathering space, following the length of the path. *Mimusops* create a backdrop for the southern end of the lawn, screening the garden from the neighboring property. Because of the ocean spray, hardy, salt-tolerant plants were essential in this part of the garden, and the *Ficus* and *Mimusops* are joined by *Coccoloba diversifolia* (pigeon plum) and *C. uvifera* (seagrape).

A large seagrape hedge marks the entire eastern property line, providing a buffer from the road. Its height is maintained to screen the road, so that, when looking out from the house, across the garden, the eye is carried to the ocean. To break up the monotony of the hedge, and allow it to act as a green "wall" in the background, lines of *Bulbine* were placed in front, with rhythmic bump-outs of *Nerium oleander* "Ice Pink" (dwarf oleander). However, the *Bulbine* did not do well in the salt spray, and was later replaced with Green Island ficus. We would one day like to place large pots at the center of each line of *Ficus*, to give the space greater depth.

On the western side of this garden, the house's large windows overlook the lawn and the ocean. Old coconut palms are placed at random and complemented by structured beds of Green Island ficus. Pigeon plums pruned to create an elevated canopy and exposed trunk are planted against the house to soften it.

ATRIUM

Greeting visitors as they enter the front door is an interior atrium with potted plants and the relaxing sound of falling water and chirping birds. Old Florida coral flooring is accented by terra-cotta tiles, and azulejo tiles line the walls and give color to the stone arches. The azulejo had aged over the years, and many pieces were weathered or broken, so we found an incredible artisan in Seville, Spain, who was able to match the originals, giving the space a fresh look.

He was also able to make a copy of a fountain in the Tropical Garden, and we placed it in the center of the courtyard. Frogs sit in each corner of the beautiful azulejo piece and spit water into the central bowl. Pots of annuals surround the fountain, and larger pots fill the corners of the courtyard. Burke's wife, Susan, loves birds, and they are housed charmingly in the courtyard in decorative colored wooden cages. The sweet sound of chirping could not be more delightful.

Potted Ficus binnendijkii *"Alii" are placed in each corner of the courtyard, and angel-wing begonias in terra-cotta pots surround the fountain.*

Begonia *"Odorata Alba"* and Farfugium japonicum *are planted along the loggia. The walls on the right are covered with vivid* Bougainvillea, *potted annuals mark the corners of the pool, and* Stephanotis *lines the balusters.*

SWIMMING POOL TERRACE AND COURTYARD

When Burke first brought us in, there was a wall running east–west just beyond the pool, ending at the stair wall of the garage. This wall cut off the pool area from the rest of the garden. As soon as we saw the site, we knew this wall was hindering the overall design and must be removed, and that gesture has shaped the garden into what it is today. By removing the wall, the pool terrace was opened to the main garden beyond, which provides a green backdrop to the terrace.

The existing pool is the one that was built with the house. The Florida coral of the terrace continues into the pool, covering the walls, floor and steps. The blue of the water creates a lovely contrast to the terrace, which provides a soft aesthetic in a large space. Large vases d'Anduze sit at each corner of the pool, planted with gardenias and surrounded by small terra-cotta pots.

Looking west, the stair wall is covered with pink bougainvillea, and decorative pots hang on the garage wall beyond, filled with ivy-leaf pelargoniums. We clad the exterior staircase with coral stone to allow it to read better with the garden. To the left, three large windows were designed by the architect Raphael Saladrigas, then of Saladrigas & Cohen Architecture, that look out from the library to the pool and garden. To the north of the pool, the kitchen walls are covered with mixed purple and magenta *Bougainvillea*, giving color and softening the facade. Natural light fills the kitchen, making it one of the most frequently used rooms in the house.

At the eastern end of the pool, a raised terrace is bordered by an interior breezeway, dividing the space from the East Lawn. Large windows on either side give views all the way to the water, and beautiful white-flowering *Cordia* trees from Texas frame the transition of the two spaces. They are among the Rosses' favorite plantings in the garden, and I would have to agree. The original Florida coral balusters delineate this area and separate it from the lower pool terrace. The space is planted with night-blooming jasmine for its intoxicating scent. More large vases d'Anduze sit in this space, planted with palms and an understory of *Asystasia gangetica* (Ganges primrose), and seating provides a quiet retreat from the pool activity. Just above is a small upper terrace with planted containers and stone balusters, and this too offers a quiet, private resting spot in the large garden—although the lower garden spaces are much preferred by the family.

To the south, a walled-in loggia runs the entire length of the house. Mediterranean-style arches break the wall and allow a closer connection between the loggia and the garden. *Caryota mitis* (fishtail palms) in containers in the loggia further connect the two spaces. Large bromeliads in terra-cotta pots are placed in the "window" of each arch, and the broad leaves of *Farfugium japonicum* and begonias soften the lower loggia wall.

Cordia boissieri *trees in bloom are underplanted with Ganges primrose.*

A pair of Solanum *trees frame the fountain, underplanted with Ganges primrose. Against the facade is a* Chamaefistula *tree, with* Clerodendrum speciosissimum *in front, and a gumbo-limbo tree (*Bursera simaruba*).*

TROPICAL GARDEN

In a change from the more formal style of the rest of the garden, this area is planted with lush, overgrown perennials and tropicals. It has less lawn and hard landscaping, so the plants can really dominate. There is a small lawn between the pool and this garden, and skewed coral stepping stones lead from the service drive to these less revealed garden spaces. The frog fountain that we reproduced for the Atrium is here, and, with its blue and white tiles, it is the focal point of this thickly planted garden. Annuals surrounded its base until it developed a leak, making the soil constantly wet and making it impossible to keep the annuals alive. As a creative solution, we planted dwarf papyrus (*Cyperus*) instead, and it is thriving in the waterlogged soil. A planting gesture that one would not think to use until presented with a situation of this kind allowed us to find a new aesthetic, and a successful one at that.

PRIVATE GARDEN

Outside of the guest suite is a courtyard furnished with chaise longues shaded by a *Lysiloma sabicu* tree. A pleached *Ficus* hedge lines the rear property wall, giving interest to it and providing screening above. Between the trunks of the hedge are two large green vases d'Anduze, elevated on coral-stone plinths and planted with tufts of Ganges primrose. A wall fountain furnished with a small basin provides white noise, its edge the perfect height for a seat or a ledge on which to place flower pots. Carved in the Dominican Republic, a coquina shell made from coral catches the water from a pair of dolphin spitters. The water spills delicately down each tier. Yellow *Solandra maxima* (chalice vine) occupies a blank wall, giving it color and softening the space. This courtyard is the perfect setting for a quiet afternoon of reading, or for evening cocktails and entertainment.

SARATOGA SPRINGS

John C. Lubischer, Senior Associate

Andre Baranowski, Photographer

We were delighted when Sheree and Marc Holliday asked us to design the garden for their newly purchased period house in Saratoga Springs, New York. This would be a second home for them. It also presented an exciting opportunity for us to design another garden for them, and to work with the same team as at their main residence, which had been a very successful partnership.

For SMI, this town is an intriguing place in which to work. It is rich in architectural styles from those of the mid-nineteenth century to just after the turn of the twentieth century. The Hollidays' house is classified as *circa* 1890 Queen Anne and Shingle architecture, since it carries elements of both styles. It is an architectural gem, but was in need of much renewal and restoration, and the Hollidays hoped to bring it back to its former glory. They had the same desire for the garden, and we were ecstatic to take up the challenge.

The house nestles on a quaint street, in a charming residential neighborhood near the world-famous Saratoga Springs horse track. Its immediate surroundings have a small-town feel, something that the family particularly prizes about Saratoga. The Hollidays are avid horse enthusiasts, and their thoroughbreds run on the track. Sheree and her daughter Daniele also often compete in jumping competitions throughout the northeast. The proximity of the Saratoga track, then—only a stroll from their new home—was perfect for them.

When we first laid eyes on the house, several elements inspired us particularly: the domed roof turret; the rustic chimney, made of local stone, that ran up the turret wall; and the white trim both inside and outside. We thought these elements, or shades of them, could be carried into the garden. We also noted the narrowness of the lot and the surrounding homes. Although resulting in a quaint feel, this would pose challenges in terms of creating screening in areas where privacy would be required.

Our hats off to the Hollidays for this successful project. They are the most gracious clients. The architect Edwin Lutyens said: "There will never be great architects or architecture without great patrons." For us, the Hollidays are great patrons. The house and garden are glorious, and we hope the family has many years of enjoyment there.

❶ FRONT GARDEN
❷ WEST GATE
❸ BACK GARDEN

Clematis climbs up the pergola, its roots shaded by low, clipped boxwood.

FRONT GARDEN

We created a plinth for the house to handle the slight change in elevation between the street and the drive that runs down the side of the house. The plinth is about 1 foot high, with slightly taller piers at the ends. Both for the practical purpose of retaining soil and for better aesthetics, the returns of the piers were designed with a sweep back toward the house. Wall and piers are made of the same rustic, native stone as the grand chimney. As an architectural element, the plinth ties the garden to the house. The stacked treatment of the stone also adds a desirable instant aged look, as if it were part of the original construction.

We designed three steps at the sidewalk, with risers made of the same rustic stone and treads of bluestone. We carried the bluestone, a favorite of the Hollidays, up the front walk and coordinated with the architect, Boris Baranovich, to use the same treatment for the elegant steps up to the newly expanded Queen Anne-like front porch, and for the pilasters that support the porch. With that, the bones of the garden and house seemed to become as one. From the street, a short carriage-path-style driveway, consisting of bluestone tracks surrounded by grass, runs along the western property line. It is just enough for one car and appears soft and gardenesque, in another reference to the era of the house.

At the front foundation and around the porch, a billowing hedge adds interest to the front landscape and serves as a special backdrop to smaller plantings. This unusual treatment involves grouping specimens of a particular plant, in various sizes, and clipping the whole to take on a pillowy, cloud-like shape. For an application such as this, along the foundation of a house, evergreens such as box or yew are the traditional choice. We selected the cold-hardy, long-lived Japanese yew *Taxus cuspidata* "Densa." It is a rich dark green and desirably soft, and suits the cloud form well. On the plinth wall, just below it, is a low, sharply clipped hedge of box, *Buxus*

The front of the house is defined by a stacked-stone plinth wall and steps, a tightly clipped hedge of green velvet boxwood (Buxus "Green Velvet"), a perennial border, and billowing Japanese yew (Taxus cuspidata "Densa").

"Green Velvet." Together with the wall, it separates the garden from the public sidewalk.

At the northeastern corner of the house, along the property line, we began the screening of the neighbor's home with *Thuja occidentalis* "Nigra" ("Nigra" arborvitae) and a staggered grouping of *Ilex* x *meserveae* Blue Princess. We positioned a green cut-leaf Japanese maple, *Acer palmatum* "Dissectum," prominently, just off the property line at the southern end of the wall. Its gracious, pendulous shape and feathery texture complete the screening of the neighboring house, just enough to make that important corner of the garden completely private. Two lilac trees are set in the grassed area between the sidewalk and street curb out front. Although they are small, ornamental trees, their presence adds a feeling of separation from the road.

With the structure of the front garden complete with hardscape, trees, hedges, and evergreen shrubs, we next filled out the beds with an additional layer of planting. These woody shrubs, perennials, ground cover, and annuals add vibrant color and texture. Beatrix Farrand (1872–1959), a revered gardener and landscape architect of the period, always said, "when placing plants, we must remember we are painting a picture,"—something she learned from her mentor, the famous English artist and gardener Gertrude Jekyll (1843–1932). Our plant palette here includes *Hibiscus syriacus* (rose of Sharon), hydrangea and *Rosa rugosa*. The perennials are geraniums, phlox, New England and New York asters, nepeta, spiderwort, sedum, Russian sage and hosta, most of which flower in shades of purple, blue, and white. The ground cover out front is the periwinkle *Vinca minor* "Bowles's Blue." The annuals, which are of a similar color scheme, are switched out three times a season, and we add touches of yellow during the summer and orange in the fall.

WEST GATE

Ideally, a garden gate should engender a sense of expectation about what is beyond. It's also the first and the last thing you see of a garden. Our gates for this garden were designed with that in mind. We made a low gate at the end of the front drive, in white AZEK, to lead into the Back Garden. We felt it was important that the gate and attached fence should be an extension of the architecture of the house, picking up on the porch columns and the white trim. The body of the gate is an arched tongue-and-groove construction, surrounded by moldings. Two similarly constructed wings are supported by sizable posts. They tie in at one end to the shingled wall of the house and at the other to the original customized fence of the same material and color. The fence, like the gate, is also tongue-and-groove, with a distinctive decorative lattice top. The Hollidays particularly liked the look of a lattice detail, but they preferred complete privacy, so that no one could peer through openings in the slats. This design conundrum was solved by sandwiching a solid AZEK panel between two lattice panels, so that the latticework appears as a relief. The result is an intricate detail that also gives the desired privacy. The fence begins at the level of the low gate and sweeps gracefully up to its full height of 6 feet. That sweep and the arch of the gate complement one another, and refer to the Queen Anne architecture of the house

Inside the gate, broken bluestone flagging leads to the mud-room door and beyond to the backyard. Importantly, this side of the property needed to be screened from the neighbor's house. We were limited by space, and so to screen windows as high as three stories up we used a combination of tall and narrow deciduous trees: fastigiate beech, the Armstrong maple (*Acer* x *freemanii* Armstrong) and the pear *Pyrus calleryana* "Cleveland Select." We underplanted these with hosta and ground cover of *Pachysandra* and periwinkle.

The back steps have stacked-stone risers and blue-stone treads, with a parapet wall of stacked stone. They are approached by a path of stepping stones with sod joints.

Beyond the pergola, with Clematis "Jackmanii Superba" on its columns, is the pool, entered via a wide set of shallow steps.

BACK GARDEN

From the gate, a broken bluestone path leads to bluestone risers with sod joints, an aesthetic link with the bluestone and rustic riser steps that lead to the main back door of the house. We worked with Boris Baranovich to design the bluestone landing, which is built within a sweeping parapet wall made of the rustic native stone. The wall flares out and then terminates at each end in a classic bulbous shape, intended to add a rustic elegance. At its base, to green it a little and divide it from the open lawn, we planted a simple bed of *Cotoneaster salicifolius* (willow-leaved cotoneaster).

A wraparound open-slat cedar-wood pergola in front of the pool house and garage is supported by heavy 8 x 8-inch cedar columns on bluestone plinths. The last set of columns at the southern end of the pergola are made of rustic stacked stone. The rim and the wooden cross members of the pergola are substantial, to allow large gaps between columns, resulting in better circulation of people and fewer obstacles to furniture. They also provide a sturdy feel, that holds up to the architecture of the house. The decorative tails of the rafters create a charming rhythm and add more comfortable shade to this area, which is paved with bluestone set on stone dust in an Ashlar pattern. It is our intention that the pergola roof will in part be covered with climbing roses and clematis, and for this purpose we placed lattice trellises of white AZEK (which is also a link to the white trim of the house). The rest of the structure will be left to weather and gray. It serves as a soft transition between the very rustic stone and the more formal white trim.

We thought it best that the pool should engage the pergola by being placed off-axis to it, and we felt a semicircle would accomplish that best. After we

explored a few versions, Sheree and Marc chose one with a small bump-out in the middle. As we often do, here we made the pool double as a fountain. This would be especially appropriate for Saratoga, which is known for its springs and fountains. The pool has five raised bluestone fountain plinths, which are one with the bluestone coping that extends into the water. The plinths are also pedestals for English lead pots that are planted with seasonal color.

The space behind the pool lent itself to a classic pleached hedge. In this style of plant training, the branches of the tree canopies are joined and tightly clipped, forming a hedge with squared-off edges. The bottom part of the hedge is open, with the trunks exposed and equally spaced. We like this form, and the way it becomes part of what we call the "bones" of the garden, and so it makes its way into many of our designs. Here, we used hornbeam trees (*Carpinus betulus*). In its form, the planting repeats and reinforces the shape of the pool, and it also screens the neighboring houses effectively. Beneath the trees is a mix of shade-loving hosta, astilbe, and climbing hydrangea, surrounded by *Pachysandra*.

The hedge is backed by a 6-foot-high wall of rustic native stone, which adds permanence, mystery, instant age, and total privacy from the alley beyond. It's also a very attractive backdrop for plants. It is clearly visible from the pool terrace and from anywhere else in the Back Garden. Along the property line from the hedge is a screen of "Nigra" arborvitae, and in front of them woody shrubs such as the beautiful large-flowering hydrangeas *H. paniculata* "Grandiflora" and "Nikko Blue." We coupled those with *Rosa rugosa*, *Nipponanthemum nipponicum* (Montauk daisies), New York and New England asters, and *Sedum* "Autumn Joy" ("Herbstfreude").

*The back gate is flanked by stacked-stone columns and walls. Seen from the alley (above, right), there is green mountain maple (*Acer saccharum *"Green Mountain") on the left and hornbeam (*Carpinus betulus*) on the right. The alley is lined with a border of* Pachysandra terminalis *ground cover, sod, and a row of northern catalpa trees (*Catalpa speciosa*).*

SHIVERICK GARDEN

Brian Vertesch, Senior Associate

Owen McGoldrick, Photographer

Betsy and Paul Shiverick contacted SMI to collaborate on a new home and garden they were planning for a property on Everglades Island in Palm Beach. There was already a house, which was to be demolished, and there were three extremely large sapodilla trees (*Manilkara zapota*) on the front property line. The estate borders a large expanse of open water between Everglades Island and Palm Beach proper. The views across the water toward Palm Beach are very pleasant, and there was no doubt that we must accentuate them as much as possible in our designs. The Shivericks explained that they were interested in developing a courtyard-style home with a very strong connection to the garden. In addition to the courtyard, they wanted to include several covered outdoor rooms that would connect different sections of the house. We spent a good deal of time discussing the courtyard and outdoor rooms, since they wanted to ensure that these architectural areas were softened with plants and connected to the gardens. This marked the beginning of an interesting and fun collaboration, as the couple stayed closely involved with all the details and decision-making.

The Shivericks had hired the architectural firm of Fairfax & Sammons to help them develop the house. Having worked with the firm before, we were quick to coordinate with them, and the concepts for house and garden moved forward apace. They were very exciting and created tremendous opportunity for tying the gardens to the house. The house is largely two stories, with a central courtyard. The entry hall is also open-air, and provides views across the courtyard, through an open garden room, to the pool garden and waterway beyond. Around the courtyard and entry hall, loggias contain decorative doors that allow access to the interior rooms. Views of the second story reveal exposed balconies, again with doors to the rooms beyond. To the south of the courtyard, a decorative balustrade separates it from the Tropical Garden.

The collaboration between the Shivericks, SMI, and Fairfax & Sammons continued smoothly and fruitfully. The teams of Tim Givens Building & Remodeling, Botanica Landscaping, and Landscape Lighting Designs executed all the designs and helped to realize the collaborators' vision for a special house and garden. The result was one of the more interesting projects to be completed on the island in recent years.

1 ENTRY GARDEN
2 COURTYARD
3 TROPICAL GARDEN
4 LIVING ROOM GARDEN
5 SWIMMING POOL GARDEN

ENTRY GARDEN

The front of the house is close enough to the road that there was not much room for us to develop an entry drive and gardens, and in fact we had to remove one of the sapodilla trees to accommodate the new driveway. Working with the architect, we developed a front wall and balustrade between the road and the proposed drive; it acts as both a decorative element and a retaining wall, helping to level the parking area. The new drive is centered on the front of the house, ensuring that the first views of the building are of the dominant facade. The drive enters the property under the dense canopy of the sapodillas and leads to an open parking court with four parking spaces, two on each side of the central axis. It is paved with elongated bricks, which are fairly common in Europe but difficult to come by in the States. At each end of the court, natural-looking massings of *Thryallis*, a shrub with yellow flowers, offset the formality.

The front facade had very strong architectural features, and we felt that it would be best displayed if we kept the foreground simple, so we created a flat plane that extends across the drive and parking to the house. To maintain this plane, instead of using shrubs against the front facade, we planted a strip of diamond *Zoysia* grass to connect the decorative stone of the water table to the drive. The result is deliberately stark, but it allows the house to dominate the entry court. On either side of the front door, a simple planting of tropical orchids and flowers in terra-cotta pots provides a small accent, further announcing the entrance.

The entry is flanked with decorative urns planted with red Pelargonium x hortorum, *surrounded by Begonia "Odorata Alba." Diamond* Zoysia *grass borders the remainder of the front facade.*

COURTYARD

The visitor discovers this wonderful space on passing through the open-air entry hall just inside the front door. The dominant front facade gives way to an area that is still formal, but much more relaxed. The courtyard is centered on a large three-tier fountain designed by the architects, surrounded by the oversized bricks that were used on the driveway. Decorative stone banding emphasizes the fountain. A collection of pots, most of which the Shivericks brought from their previous garden, cluster around it, housing a collection of plants that softens the courtyard and creates the feeling of a garden. *Bougainvillea* in pots on the second-story balcony cascades over the rail toward the courtyard below. It adds an exciting burst of color, as well as softening the architecture and adding to the garden effect.

The courtyard is lined on three sides by loggias and a large outdoor room that separates the courtyard from the pool. The fourth side is relatively open, with only a low balustrade separating it from the Tropical Garden beyond.

Right: The Courtyard contains a variety of decorative containers. Bougainvillea *"New River" provides a burst of brilliant color, and* Trachelospermum jasminoides *is trained on the wall in a diamond pattern.*

Opposite: The Tropical Garden is anchored by a Ficus aurea *tree.* *Alocasia "Calidora,"* Heliconia caribae x bihai *"Hot Rio Nights,"* Philodendron *"Burle Marx," and* Asystasia gangetica *combine to create a lush perimeter. Coral flagstones with Zoysia grass joints provide a walkway through, skirting the bed of pink begonias at the bottom of the tree.*

TROPICAL GARDEN

This area is anchored by a very large *Ficus aurea* tree that was trucked from North Miami. The tree towers over the house, and its trunk is about 8 feet in diameter. Its immensity has given the house and courtyard an immediate feeling of history, and its large canopy provides shade and shelter, allowing us to dramatically expand the plant palette in this garden. Using a collection of large-leaved tropicals such as *Heliconia*, ginger, and *Alocasia*, we created layers of foliage from the roofline to the garden path. Reinforcing the move away from the formal courtyard, the path into the Tropical Garden is of coral flagstones separated by grass joints. It leads to a small fountain tucked into the hedge at the property line. The fountain is visible from many rooms of the house, and, just as the central courtyard fountain does, it fills the air with the soft sound of water. Pink *Begonia semperflorens* are planted between the path and the base of the *Ficus* tree; they are low-growing enough that the tree roots remain prominent, and they produce an attractively soft, cloudy effect at the foot of the tree.

LIVING ROOM GARDEN

On the opposite side of the house from the Tropical Garden, and opening off the living room, this garden is more private than the courtyard garden on the other side of the living room, and is also smaller. From the living room, the main view is of a wall fountain. A row of pleached *Ilex* (holly) trees screens the neighboring property from view from both the first and second floors of the Shivericks' house. The part of the house that this garden borders is two stories tall, and it feels large when seen from the space. To reduce the massing, *Trachelospermum jasminoides* (Confederate jasmine) is trained over parts of the first-floor wall. The vines are interrupted by an antique mask, and as they grow, the wall will disappear and only the face will be visible. The vines and adjacent trees veil the entire Living Room Garden in foliage. The paving here differs from that of the main courtyard, being mostly limestone with no brick. To create variety and interest in the paving, we added a band of pebbles laid on end, which frames the central terrace area. At both ends of the garden, decorative wooden gates allow access to the family parking and the Swimming Pool Gardens respectively.

This page: Podocarpus macrophyllus *hedges enclose the terrace and direct the view to the* Thrinax radiata *palms flanking a coral flagstone walkway that leads to a decorative urn on its pedestal. Under the antique mask,* Begonia *"Odorata Alba" and* Blechnum gibbum *"Silver Lady" spill on to the paving.*

Opposite: Phoenix canariensis *palms create an allée on the long axis of the pool, and* Zoysia *grass was planted over the concrete dock to extend the garden.*

SWIMMING POOL GARDEN

As are so many gardens with pools, this one is centered on the swimming pool. In developing this area, we found that we had the opportunity to take advantage of a borrowed view by continuing the neighbor's *allée* of *Phoenix canariensis* (Canary Island date palm) across the pool gardens. As a bonus, we had done the neighbor's garden many years earlier, and so we were able to please two clients by creating the borrowed vista.

The view from the house to the waterway beyond is stunning, and there was no sense in competing with such natural beauty, so we kept the Swimming Pool Garden simple. Two plinths, one at each end of the garden on the central pool axis, are topped with antique olive jars. Since the garden is so simple overall, we felt additional ornament was needed, and were able to use several iron pots that the Shivericks had at another property. They are planted with red pelargoniums, providing a dramatic burst of color while fitting into the unfussy design.

One design element that had a large impact on the pool garden was the grass dock. After the pool was developed by the architect, we realized that the space between it and the dock would be very narrow. Our solution was to increase the size of the lot. The Shivericks had always planned to have a dock, and so we created one that joins seamlessly to the lawn of the garden, topped with the same grass as the pool garden, rather than with stone or wood. In a town where the price of waterfront real estate is extremely high, we not only created a much more comfortable garden space, but also added a considerable amount of valuable land.

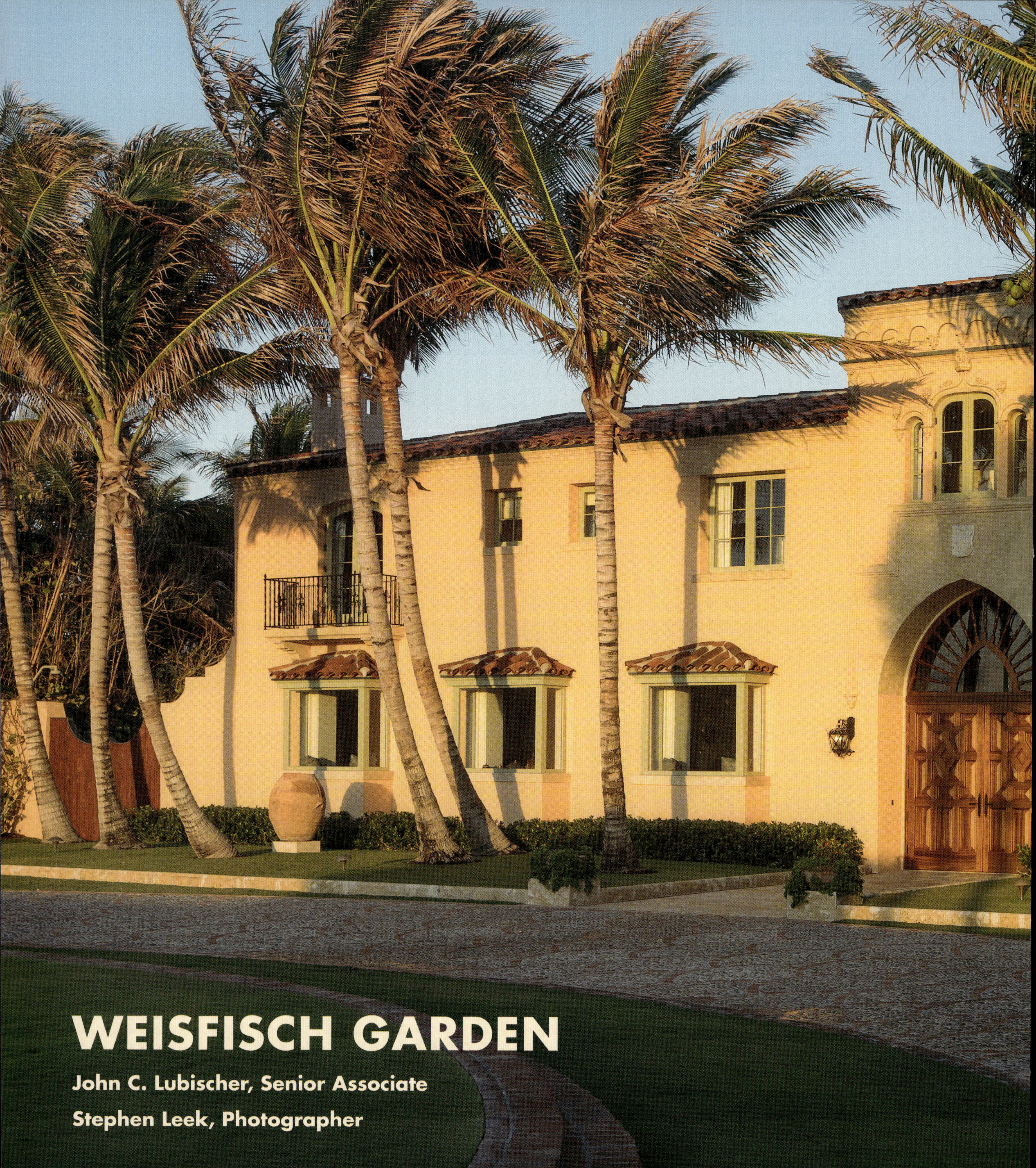

WEISFISCH GARDEN

John C. Lubischer, Senior Associate

Stephen Leek, Photographer

Uniquely, this Landmark Mediterranean-style seaside house in Palm Beach was designed by not one, but two of the local all-time architectural greats of the early twentieth century: Addison Mizner and Maurice Fatio. Mizner designed the main part of the house, with its grand front entry, in 1923. Just five years later, Fatio was commissioned to add wings to the north and south ends of the house.

Pnina and Yoram Weisfisch subsequently took on the restoration and remodeling of the ninety-year-old house. Their desire was to update it spectacularly, to expand it and make it more suitable for their large extended family, while remaining true to its history. For this task they commissioned the prolific Palm Beach architect Jacqueline Albarran. The Weisfischs knew, as did Jackie, that the restoration could not be complete unless the details of the garden were as spectacular as both Mizner and Fatio would have wanted. The Palm Beach Landmarks Preservation Commission would also need to approve all architectural details of house and garden. Jackie introduced SMI to the Weisfischs and we were selected for the job, with high expectations. Through the combined effort of owners, architects, designers, and installers, this successful project was granted the prestigious Ballinger Award by the Palm Beach Preservation Foundation.

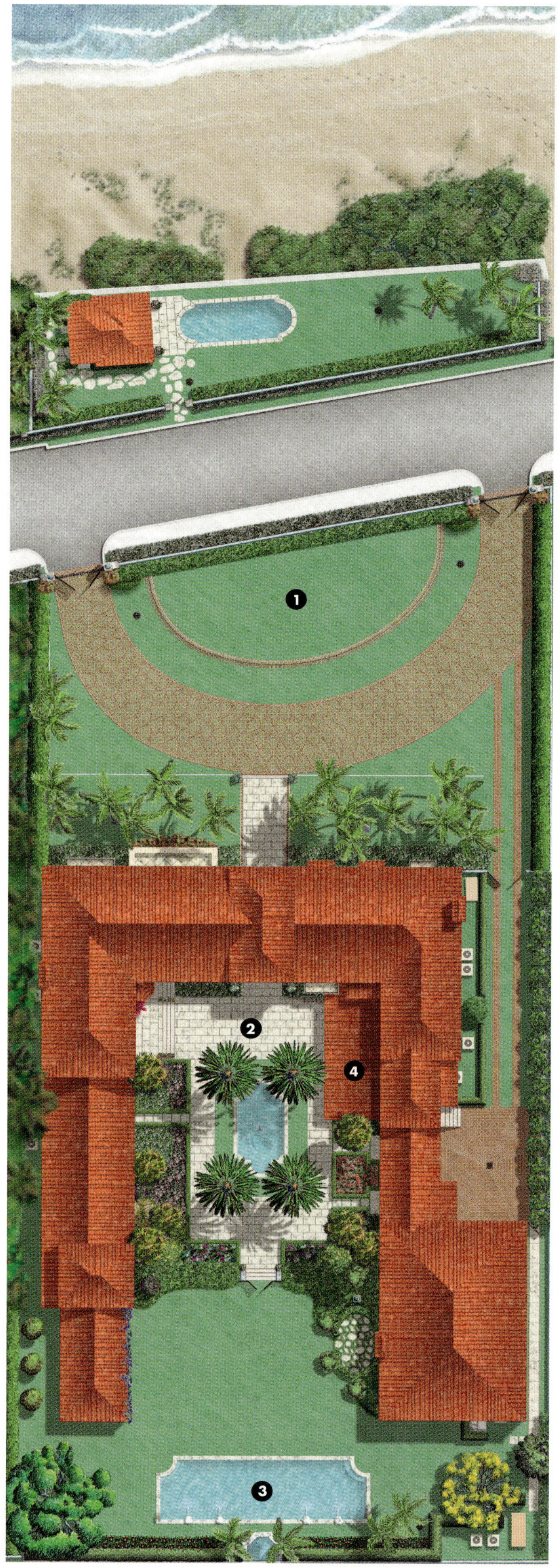

1. ENTRANCE, MOTOR COURT AND FRONT GARDEN
2. COURTYARD
3. POOL
4. LOGGIA AND SITTING GARDEN

ENTRANCE, MOTOR COURT AND FRONT GARDEN

Masterful coquina-carved pilasters frame the two entrances to the drive, with wrought-iron gates made after an original drawing by Mizner. The Weisfischs requested proper circulation for cars, and ample parking for family gatherings. The house is very close to the street, so we had to balance the requirement for hard surface with landscaping to soften it. There were also Town requirements for open green space, and the problem of how to drain the drive away from the front of the house, which is lower than the street. This had been a problem at least since the road was asphalted. Juggling all this, we designed a gardenesque motor court between two landscaped areas, and a semicircular drive leading from one entrance to the other.

A shoulder of reinforced sod runs alongside a circulation lane of similar width, both for drainage and to park several cars. A two-step raised curb of old Chicago brick along its eastern edge leads to an elevated lawn. A carved limestone curb designates the parking area. Such details transform the space from typical circular drive to motor court.

For the surface, we first considered a traditional treatment of coquina slabs with sod joints, common in Palm Beach for historic drives. It would look soft and help with drainage, and the Landmarks Preservation Commission would approve. But Pnina wanted something more detailed, although she wasn't sure

Looking east to the courtyard and back entrance of the house through the garden gate and Phoenix sylvestris *palms.*

what. We always listen carefully to and interpret our clients' desires, and that something for the drive turned out to be a mosaic of river stones. We had shown one to Pnina that we had designed for another project in nearby Lost Tree. So as not to duplicate it, we explored various patterns, and Pnina and her daughter Monique chose a fish-scale design. Old Chicago brick banding ties the drive back to the curb of the parking area, and the field is of beige, tan and brownish stones set closely in mortar. We always insist on the right individual setting of each river stone, and we never use those that come set on prefabricated sheets. For it to look correct, the artisanry must be true, just as it would be installed on a street in Granada, Spain. However, this required expanding the budget considerably (one reason we did not suggest it at first), and caused some delay. Although the family had wanted the project to be completed fast, they accepted the extra cost and time. The result is a stunning, distinctive drive, with each stone placed meticulously by the master mason Harry Gilbert.

The front entrance and coquina curb, with its plinth, pots, and swaying coconuts. Low Ficus microcarpa *"Green Island" grows along the front foundation.*

A magnificent view to the courtyard from the front entry walk, through the house, and beyond to the pool and west fountain.

COURTYARD

The courtyard's central fountain had fallen into disrepair, so we restored the interior and kept the original coquina coping intact, with all its worn imperfections. Sylvester date palms (*Phoenix sylvestris*) at each corner of the fountain frame it symmetrically, their loose canopy creating just the right kind of dappled shade. This was where we wanted a good show of color. The tall part of the house to the east and the lower wings to the north and south protect this area from the ocean winds, allowing us to use many diverse flowering plants. Beds contain woody shrubs, *Thrinax* palms, bougainvillea, flowering perennials, and ground cover. At the western end of the courtyard is an original set of charming coquina steps, as worn as the coping on the fountain. We chose to keep them intact, too. We removed a masonry wall that flanked them (it was not original to the garden, but had been added in recent years when a pool was built just west of the steps), and replaced it with a steep slope, covered by a billowing hedge of Green Island ficus. The natural green massing, with its undulating shape, was a much more pleasing way to handle the change of grade.

The coquina steps called for a gate, both for aesthetic reasons and for safety. It must be made of aluminum, not wrought iron, because of corrosion from the salt-laden winds, but we felt strongly that it must also look as delicate as possible. It is truly a challenge to create a gate and maintain proper structure using thin aluminum members. Understanding our limitations, we charetted the possibilities and the present gate design emerged, with its pleasingly ethereal swirls flanked by sturdy, ornate posts reminiscent of the Mizner front entrance gate.

Below: Beyond the garden gate is the pool with its original shell fountain.

Right: The central courtyard fountain, with its original coquina coping, is surrounded by diamond Zoysia grass and Phoenix sylvestris *palms. Beyond is the perennial border, backed with a hedge of* Ficus microcarpa *"Green Island."*

Beyond the pool, with its plinths and coquina-rubble pots, is an original coquina fountain set in a screen of little-leaf clusia (C. guttifera), with tall coconut palms.

POOL

The existing pool did not suit the architecture of the house, and we felt that its position cut off the garden; it was out of place. It was removed, and a new one built toward the western property line. This created an expanse of grass between courtyard and pool that would accommodate a play area (an item on the Weisfischs' wishlist). The green expanse also created a void that gave instant depth to the backyard. We felt the pool should be long and fountain-like, and that it should refer to the Mizner and Fatio details of the original design. Of course, we would add our own flair. (When we design a garden for a Landmark house, we find it a great compliment when people cannot distinguish between the original elements and the new.) We wanted to tie the pool visually to the original coquina fountain in front of the western property wall. We designed four classically shaped pilasters from which water could shoot out into the pool, with urns on top for annuals. The coquina-rubble urns make a striking contrast with the smooth coquina pool walls.

LOGGIA AND SITTING GARDEN

Jackie had designed two loggias, one in the courtyard and the other off the north wing of the house, near the pool. They were welcome additions to the original architecture, as was the balcony overlook and other details that she added. *Pyrostegia venusta* (Florida flame vine) is working its way to the top of the pool loggia, and will cover it in just a few years. For the seating area below the balcony overlook, off the south wing of the house, we turned the original indoor fireplace chimney to make an outdoor fireplace terrace. It is partly screened by *Psidium cattleianum* (cattley guava) overhead and at eye level, and by Green Island ficus at its lower level. It is a place for quiet conversation, or to read a book or simply contemplate.

The loggia opens onto the courtyard, with central fountain and perennial beds.

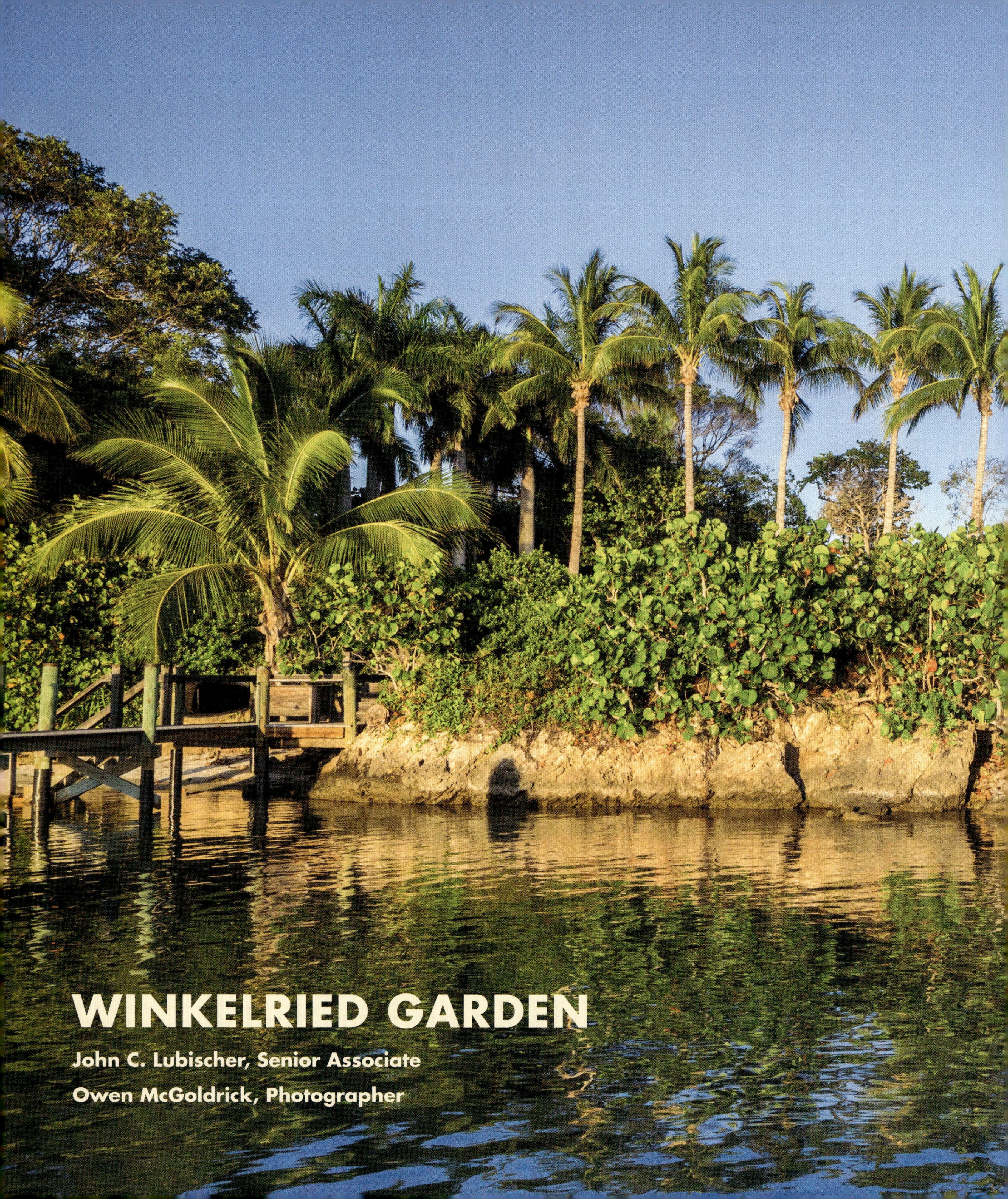

WINKELRIED GARDEN

John C. Lubischer, Senior Associate

Owen McGoldrick, Photographer

We were thrilled when the interior designer Victoria Hagan (with whom we had worked in the past very successfully) invited us to join her on this project. We were eager to team up with her again, and also with the architects, Ferguson & Shamamian, an excellent firm whose reputation precedes it. The clients, Jon and Abby Winkelried, were a delight to work for. After learning their tastes, we were off and running on a design that would be both fully functional and aesthetically pleasing.

Jupiter Island is a narrow spit of land between the Atlantic Ocean and the Intracoastal Waterway, north of Palm Beach. It is naturally pristine and has, at least in part, been preserved by the Town policy of screening views of homes from the road and from one another. This requirement represented a welcome opportunity for us to create a privacy screening for the property, consisting of a pleasing combination of various species.

At SMI it is one of our goals to tie the garden back to the house from the interior out. Views and finishes are all very important. The result of our efforts here is the harmony between natural and structural elements that our clients desired, and which they will be able to enjoy for years to come.

1 FRONT GARDEN
2 SIDE GARDEN
3 ABBY'S OFFICE GARDEN
4 WEST GARDEN
5 WATERFRONT

Coconut palms lean over the coquina-stone ledge that borders the Intracoastal Waterway.

*The softly winding drive approaches the Motor Court. The lawn is dotted with curved-trunk coconut palms (*Cocos nucifera*), and beyond are* Ficus nitida *trees.*

FRONT GARDEN

Two large seagrape trees (*Coccoloba uvifera*) flank the main entrance to the property, from where a softly curving gravel drive approaches the house through the front grounds. As part of the screening of the neighbors to north and south, and for interest, we incorporated a grove of citrus and other fruit trees. There was a large banyan tree (*Ficus benghalensis*), interesting in form, which we retained as a feature along the drive. The client wanted the grounds to have a loose, relaxed feel, and we decided that there was no better way to achieve that than with sweeping coconut palms (*Cocos nucifera*). We planted a generous number along the main entry drives and in the front lawn.

In front of the house is a motor court, for both form and function. It serves as a parking hub that leads to the front entrance door, the guesthouse, and the service area (which has a separate drive). To the east and south side of the motor court entry are four *Ficus nitida* trees that we moved from elsewhere on the site. They shield the house from the approach and from any other possible views from the road. We brought in a white orchid tree (*Bauhinia alba*) to screen the guesthouse from view, and a purple one (*B.* x *blakeana*) to screen the service area. Loose hedges of *Viburnum* beneath the trees and around the motor court compartmentalize the space naturally. The walk to the front door is of French limestone, the stone of choice for all the formal walkways, steps, terraces, and walls on the property. The lawn on either side is slightly elevated from the motor court, with a low retaining wall and two steps. Coconut palms grace the grassy areas, and two lead pots filled with *Jasminum officinale* "Netty" flank the door.

SIDE GARDEN

From the service court a shell tabby path leads westward toward the dock and the Intracoastal. Its first destination is a small viewing garden, with a limestone terrace where the various trees, shrubs, and flowers can be enjoyed at close proximity. At the entrance is a *Bougainvillea arborea* (tree bougainvillea), which blooms magnificently with purple flowers throughout much of the year and in particular during the cooler months, when the Winkelrieds are in residence. It has a falling form that arches toward the terrace and over the stepping stones that lead through the garden from a side door of the house. In the sunny area near the terrace there is grass between the stepping stones, and in the shade we used Australian violet (*Viola hederacea*). A *Psidium cattleianum* (cattley guava) with a cinnamon-colored trunk anchors the back part of the garden. The orchids that hang in its branches are visible from the kitchen and living-room windows, as are glimpses of much of the other plantings here. *Farfugium*, *Blechnum gibbum* (silver lady ferns) and *Rhapis* palms give texture and body, and for color there is *Spathiphyllum* (flowering ginger) and a variety of perennials in a good mix of white, pale pink, purples, and blues.

ABBY'S OFFICE GARDEN

The shell tabby path next reaches Abby's Office Garden. We planted a perennial bed with an English-style color scheme of blue, purple, and white perennials that Gertrude Jekyll would have been proud of. It includes *Stachytarpheta* (porterweed), blue and white plumbago, *Salvia* "Indigo Spires" and Mystic Spires Blue ("Balsalmisp"), *Barleria cristata* (Philippine violet), purple and white *Angelonia*, and *Evolvulus glomeratus* (blue daze). It is a pleasing blend of Abby's favorite colors, and clearly visible from her office. It can also be seen from other windows in the house, and from the upper deck, both loggias, and the pool terraces.

From the edge of the perennial garden, with its soft planting in purple and white, both the pool loggia and the living room loggia can be seen.

*Opposite: The lower lawn, with its grouping of royal palms (*Roystonia regia*) and seagrape trees (*Coccoloba uvifera*), a billowing hedge of* Ficus microcarpa *"Green Island" and plantings of* Philodendron *"Burle Marx."*

Top: The south loggia overlooks the upper-level lawn of diamond Zoysia *grass studded with coconut palms.*

Above: The natural coquina ledge, topped with Clematis terniflora *"Tropical Wonder," borders the mid-level Great Lawn.*

WEST GARDEN

At SMI, we work as much as we can with the natural lay of the land. This house is set on the highest part of the property, with two roomy loggias on the garden side, and the grounds at the back incorporate a welcome elevation change, which lends itself to a multi-tier effect in the garden.

The limestone loggias form the first tier of the garden. The pool—a simple, sizable rectangle, as the client wished—and its surrounding terrace are on the second tier, which was created by adding a small limestone-clad retaining wall and four steps leading down from the north loggia.

The south loggia opens to a level expanse of lawn with many coconut palms. A stepping-stone path winds its way south toward Jon's office. For that spot we selected an interestingly formed white *Cordia sebestena* (geiger tree), which flowers profusely on and off throughout the year. At the northern end of the upper lawn, a small grass path leads down to the pool terrace.

Off the west pool terrace is a staggered row of coconut palms, their fronds drooping over the pool and the lawn below. We brought in two large specimen seagrape trees—character pieces—and placed one at the northern end of the pool and the other on the eastern side. The one to the north stands proud of a group of *Roystonia regia* (royal palm) and a hedge of mahoe (*Hibiscus tiliaceus*) and other screening plantings. Three yellow *Tabebuia argentea* trees between the pool and loggia are underplanted with *Carissa macrocarpa* (Natal plum).

West of the pool, we exposed a ledge of naturally occurring coquina stone about 4 feet in depth. *Clematis terniflora* "Tropical Wonder" flows over the top of the ledge. By leveling the land west from the bottom of the ledge, we were able to create what we call the Great Lawn. This necessary open green space gives depth to the magnificent view from the house or loggias to the Intracoastal and beyond. It is also a useful flat expanse for a tent event, if desired. All this leveling of the slope resulted in a sizable drop-off at the edge of the Intracoastal, and that required us to create the tallest of the coquina ledges.

WATERFRONT

When I am working on a property, I often find something that triggers my imagination and causes me to run to my design table to put pencil to paper. Here it was the natural coquina ledge, with its crags and its weather-eroded roughness, near the dock. It was partly submerged and, depending on the tide, extended above the water by 9 or 10 feet. It inspired us to design a continuation of it, along with two sets of carved coquina boulder steps. The boulders we used were excavated from the site, and some weighed up to 18 tons. The carved coquina steps to the north wind down to a small beach of white sand not far from the dock. The second set of steps, about halfway down the western property line, are Venetian in style, in that they enter the water. Jon enjoys watersports, and both sets of steps therefore have a practical purpose as well as an aesthetic one. The ledge itself also serves a most important purpose: protecting the property from erosion into the Intracoastal during storms or unusual tides. I did enjoy directing the placement of all the boulders, sometimes even standing in the water to do so.

The final touch to any project is always the planting. We added a grove of royal palms just east of the Venetian steps, and a good number of coconuts, some with heavy sweeps along the boulder ledge. The *Ficus microcarpa* "Green Island" above the ledge is allowed to grow over it in some places. Purple *Ipomoea pes-caprae* (railroad vine) in some of the cracks of the rocks and yellow-flowering *Wedelia* are both helpful in preventing soils from eroding in difficult places like this. A hammock of specimen-size seagrape trees on the slope between the house and the great lawn are trimmed to appear windswept, their canopies touching.

WORTH AVENUE

Brian Vertesch, Senior Associate

Owen McGoldrick, Photographer

At the risk of sounding iconoclastic, I have included a public project in this book. These projects are not the mainstay of the firm, although we do occasionally accept such commissions—that is to say, when we know we can make a difference. With this one, we felt we could.

Worth Avenue, in the heart of Palm Beach, stretches from the Atlantic Ocean west toward Lake Worth, and is lined by several buildings that date back to the avenue's humble beginnings as a dirt road, as well as some of the world's most luxurious shops. In 2007, we were presented with the opportunity to restore it, and in fact we nearly declined it. We were asked to be the resident representative for an Italian firm. We had never done that (and never have since), but I was persuaded to go to a meeting with the three largest real-estate owners on Worth Avenue. However, after being shown what was presented to the group, I politely bowed out.

A few days later I was asked, privately, what I thought of the presentation. Confidentially, I said it was pure kitsch, and would never be approved by the town of Palm Beach. Worth Avenue was in a sad state of aged, neglected disrepair, but what was shown at that meeting was irreverent. SMI was then asked to prepare a schematic showing what we would propose. We accepted the challenge.

The restoration began with numerous meetings with merchant groups, civic associations, the Garden Club of Palm Beach, the Fire Department, the Police Department, Town Commissioners, and officials. The design team also kept an "open door" policy, and offered to meet and present the project to any group or citizen who had concerns or comments about it. This massive effort to include as many people as possible in the development not only helped to create a design that addressed more of the community's concerns, but also allowed the community to feel involved and to "own" the project.

The goal was to provide a safe and comfortable shopping district and to revive the glamour that made Worth Avenue one of the world's most famous shopping destinations. Driven by the goals set out by the merchants and the community, the design has corrected many hazards and much of the discomfort that had been created for pedestrians over the years through neglect and outdated traffic design. The introduction of majestic coconut palms all along the street creates the shade that the avenue lacked. The avenue is also now unified, an identifiable district from end to end, while its historical significance to the town of Palm Beach is respected. Through the use and repetition of plants, paving design, and pocket parks, SMI has created a shady, safe, comfortable, and visually stimulating

The eastern entrance to Worth Avenue is marked by pilasters and tall coconut palms.

1. EASTERN ENTRANCE
2. TRIANGLE PARK
3. COLONNADES
4. VIA PARIGI
5. HIBISCUS PLAZA

WORTH
AVENUE
WORTH
AVENUE

1
2

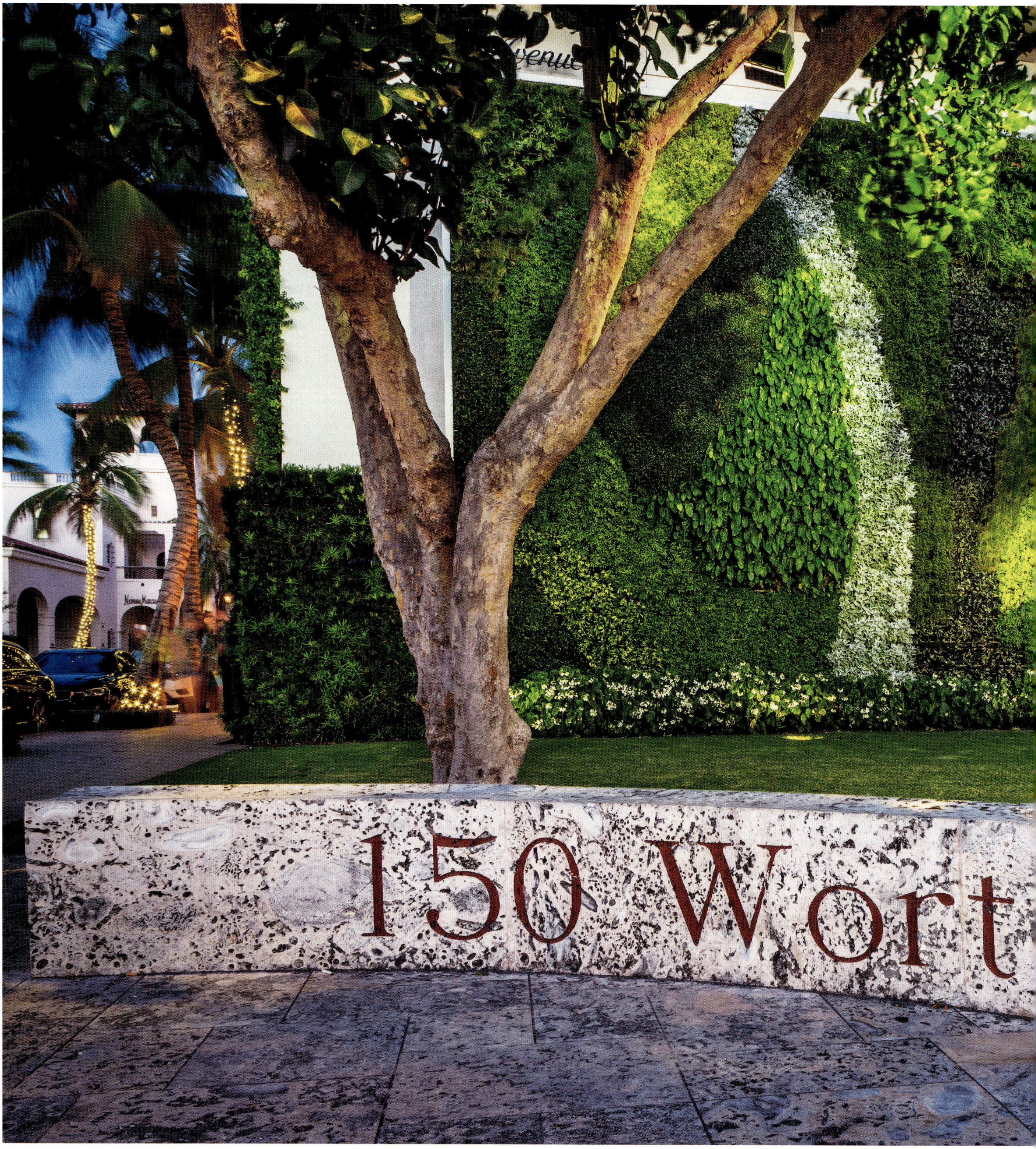
150 Wort

environment that will leave lasting memories for visitors.

Drawing on historical research into Worth Avenue and Palm Beach, the design developed to incorporate themes used by the town's most famous architect, Addison Mizner—who was also one of the first architects to work on the avenue—and the coconut palm that helped to give birth to the name of the island. The paving for the main corridors incorporates a native Floridian shell to create a tabby concrete that is unique to the avenue, and which, when combined with designed control (or expansion) joints, blends seamlessly with the historic buildings. During the design process, several areas along the avenue were identified as unused and were modified to create pocket parks, providing pedestrian connections and destinations. Further unifying the avenue, as well as increasing safety, many pedestrian crosswalk nodes were introduced, as were shady trees and benches that provide an oasis from both pedestrian and vehicular traffic.

The redesign of the avenue was completed in 2010 and encompasses a combination of luxury and old-world restraint that has resulted in understated elegance. Drawing on its history and on the community's desire to make it more pedestrian-friendly, the refurbished avenue will be able to carry into the future the "Worth Avenue Experience" that has been cherished by shoppers for a century.

*A living wall forms the back of the triangle park, with a coquina bench and pigeon plum trees (*Coccoloba diversifolia*).*

The elegant facades of Worth Avenue are enhanced by the tall coconut palms, and the rhythm of the colonnades echoed in the clipped evergreen columns.

Via Parigi leads off Worth Avenue. SMI Landscape Architecture undertook the design of this space several years before the rest of the street.

VIA PARIGI

Hibiscus Plaza was formerly an unsightly side street. The trees are Tabebuia impetiginosa, *and the terminal bench is set under a pergola draped with blue trumpet vine,* Thunbergia grandiflora.

STOP

PROJECT CREDITS

Casa Bendita
Architect: Peacock + Lewis Architects and Planners
Builder: Hedrick Brothers
Landscape contractor: The Lopez Group
Stonework: Herpel Cast Stone
Landscape lighting: Landscape Lighting Designs
Latticework: Yonder Woodworks
Planters: Mecox Gardens

Fisher Garden
Architects: John Volk (original); Clemens Bruns Schaub (renovation)
Builder: Worth Builders
Stonework: Palm Beach Cast Stone
Landscape contractor: Botanica Landscaping
Landscape lighting: Landscape Lighting Designs
Pots: Seibert & Rice

El Lido
Architects: August Geiger (original); Jacqueline Albarran (restoration and additions)
Builder: Tim Givens Building & Remodeling (superintendent Saul Irving)
Landscape contractor: Botanica Landscaping
Landscape lighting: Orsman Design
Stone fountain carving: Traditional Cut Stone
Antique tile: L'Antiquario Antique Tile

Mautner Garden
Architect: Kenneth Dowd
Builder: RFG General Contractors
Landscape contractor: Sages Mclean & Company

Nason Garden
Architect: Portuondo Perotti Architects
Builder: Ramon Garcia
Landscape contractor: Corlett Landscape Architecture
Stonework: Geo Olazabal
Landscape lighting: Landscape Lighting Designs
Tabby concrete: Connery Concrete

Patterson Garden
Architects: Addison Mizner (original); Bridges Marsh & Associates (renovation)
Builder: Hedrick Brothers
Landscape contractor: Nanak's Landscaping
Stonework: Herpel Cast Stone
Landscape lighting: Landscape Lighting Designs
Tile artisan: Dan Droney

Peterffy Garden
Architect: Dan Kahan of Smith & Moore Architects
Builder: Woolems
Landscape contractor: The Lopez Group
Teak dock: Vern Mowrey of the Yacht Shop
Boardwalk: Construction Technology
Tabby concrete driveway: Connery Concrete
Specimen trees: Sean Jacobus Trees

Plumb Garden
Architect: John Milner Architects
Building contractor: C. Raymond Davis
Swimming pool contractor: Ehrich & Ehrich Landscape Architects
Landscape installation: Ehrich & Ehrich Landscape Architects and Accents of Nature Landscaping
Stonemason: Ehrich & Ehrich Landscape Architects
Lighting: Orsman Design

Rakolta Garden
Architect: Bridges Marsh & Associates
Building contractor: Walbridge
Landscape contractor: Botanica Landscaping
Lighting contractor: Landscape Lighting Designs
Pots: Authentic Provence
Paving: M&J Pavers and Stone
Metal arches: Miller's Custom Metals
Metalwork: Reich Metal Fabricators

La Salona
Architects: Marion Sims Wyeth (original, 1926); Maurice Fatio (addition, 1929); Raphael Saladrigas (renovation)
Builder: Seaspray Group
Stonework: Prestige Architectural Stone
Landscape contractor: Jesse Casserino Landscape and Botanica Landscaping
Azulejo tile: Cerámica Artística Sevillana – Antonio Gonzalez

Saratoga Springs
Architect: Boris Baranovich
Building contractor: Hobbs
Landscape installation: Dom's Landscaping
Stonemason: Upstate Rock
Pergola: New Energy Works
Custom fence contractor: Interstate Lumber

Shiverick Garden
Architect: Fairfax & Sammons
Builder: Tim Givens Building & Remodeling
Landscape contractor: Botanica Landscaping
Landscape lighting: Landscape Lighting Designs

Weisfisch Garden
Architects: Addison Mizner (original, 1923); Maurice Fatio (additions, 1928); Jacqueline Albarran (renovation)
Owner reps: Andy Pizey and Tim Mckim
Building contractor: Worth Builders
Stonemason: Harry Gilbert
Installation of driveway mosaic: Harry Gilbert
Landscape installation: Rood Landscape
Metalwork: Reich Metal Fabricators
Lighting contractor: Landscape Lighting Designs

Winkelried Garden
Architect: Ferguson & Shamamian
Builder: Hedrick Brothers
Landscape installation: Rood Landscape
Stone contractor: Exterior Expressions of Florida
Specimen trees: Sean Jacobus Trees
Tabby concrete walks: Connery Concrete

Worth Avenue
Architect (clock tower): Mark Marsh of Bridges Marsh & Associates
Builder: Burkhardt Construction
Landscape contractor: Valley Crest
Landscape lighting: Landscape Lighting Designs
Stone fountain carving: Traditional Cut Stone
Fountain and pergola contractors: Hedrick Brothers and Hackl Pool Construction Co.
Living wall: GSky Plant Systems
Tabby concrete walks: Connery Concrete
Custom lanterns: Urban Electric

INDEX

Page numbers in *italic* refer to the illustrations

First published 2018 by Merrell Publishers Limited, London and New York

Merrell Publishers Limited
70 Cowcross Street
London EC1M 6EJ

merrellpublishers.com

British Library Cataloguing in Publication data:
A catalogue record for this book is available from the British Library.

ISBN 978-1-8589-4672-6

Produced by Merrell Publishers Limited
Designed by Nicola Bailey
Edited by Rosanna Fairhead
Proofread by Marion Moisy
Indexed by Hilary Bird

Printed and bound in China

Jacket, front: Fisher Garden (pages 23–35)

Jacket, back, from top: Peterffy Garden (pages 86–99); Shiverick Garden (pages 156–65); Plumb Garden (pages 101–15)

Frontispiece: Winkelried Garden (pages 180–93)

Page 4: Patterson Garden (pages 73–85)

Page 6: La Salona (pages 130–41)